Prayer as a Force

By

A. Maude Royden

Author of "Sex and Common Sense,"
"Political Christianity," etc.

G. P. Putnam's Sons
New York & London
The Knickerbocker Press
1923

Published, January, 1923
Reprinted, April, 1923

Made in the United States of America

DEDICATED TO

THE LITTLE COMPANY

WITH WHOM I HAVE

SOUGHT TO FIND

GOD IN PRAYER

PREFATORY NOTE

THESE addresses were delivered on Sunday evenings at the Kensington Town Hall and Eccleston Guildhouse, and do not form a perfectly consecutive course. The greater number, however, were given as a series, and the others are sufficiently connected in substance and principle to be in place in the same book. The point of view they suggest is that prayer is (at least) as real and living a force in the world as any of the great forces revealed to us by Natural Science. It seems to most of us capricious and unreliable for the same reason that (for example) electricity seemed so to a world which knew it only as flashes of lightning or sparks from a black cat: namely, that we do not understand its nature or its laws. When we do so we shall be able to pray with power, as Christ did and all the saints in their degree. We shall share His perfect confidence and we shall understand that we "have not because we ask not."

A. M. R.

June, 1922.

CONTENTS

PRAYER AS A FORCE

WORSHIP

IT is fashionable nowadays to say that you can have religion without God and that the earliest forms of religion did not have any God. I suppose that is true if one thinks of God always as a person. I think Miss Jane Harrison, in her latest publication, is obviously right when she says that it is possible to be religious, and that people have done religious acts and had a religion when they had no God. If she means—and I think it is clear that she does mean—"when they have no personal God," I agree with her. She says the first beginnings of religion were generally some form of magic, and that magic does not imply a god at all in the sense of a person. Magic is an effort on the part of the magician to use some kind of power to bring about the things that men mostly desire—a good harvest, success, sun or rain, or fertility in the tribe, or victory in battle, or any of those first things that all human beings desire, and which they have a sort of feeling some people can get for them. By some kind of magic, by hearing some sort of a conjurer, by going through certain rites, by drawing lots, by imitating the thing that you want to happen, you can perhaps make it happen. And she says, and I repeat it seems to me quite rightly, that these acts are religious acts, but they do not imply a god, at least not a person.

Of course, it all depends on our idea of what God is, and most of us have got so strongly hold of the idea of a personal God that when Jane Harrison says these things can be done without any God we think, Yes, that is quite right, they can be done without a Person. But they cannot be done without a belief on the part of those who do them that they are invoking some power that is invisible, that is really spiritual, and that is stronger than they are themselves. All magic, I think, implies that. Some people have a certain gift, perhaps, which enables them to heal, or some kind of wisdom in using herbs; or they want a good harvest and they think some medicine man or conjurer can get it for them. Sometimes, I think, these magicians are aware that they are using a power which is not exactly themselves. It is something beyond themselves, a spiritual power, therefore the act they do is a religious act. Only I would say that that perception of a spiritual power which they do not understand, which works rather capriciously, but which they always hope they can conciliate or bribe or deceive—because a great many magical feats are based upon an attempt to deceive—that power does really exist; and I would say that that power of God is, to the magician—though he would never call it by such a name—an operative cause. If you do certain things certain results will follow; but then, in my philosophy, the cause of this is God, because God is the operative cause behind all creation. Personality is, in my creed, one of the attributes of God, but I would never say a person had not a god because he had not a personal God. But I think it is perfectly true to say this is not realised by the magician. I think very often he does not realise what it is that he does.

Some of you will have read Browning's great poem about Mr. Sludge, the medium, in which a fraudulent spiritualistic medium admits his fraud, and yet he says, "All the same there was some truth in it. Of course, I couldn't help deceiving people; they were asking to be deceived, but all the same there was something there"; an impression I suppose most of us get when we hear of fraudulent mediums. There have been many fraudulent mediums, but all the same isn't there something there? And so with these magicians, although many of them may have been frauds—because it is very difficult to be a magician without deceiving somebody—yet they knew there was something there, and that was their first primitive idea of God. It is not worship, but religion, and worship comes later. Worship comes when the nature of these powers becomes partly known to us. Behind the power that makes the harvest, that sends the rain or sun, or makes the tribe have many children or gives it success in war: behind this power of evading God, of getting round him, or bribing or frightening him, it may be, (because all these things are resorted to by primitive religions), there is something which is constant, which is trustworthy, and I feel that no one knows better perhaps than the magician himself that underneath all the chances he takes, and underneath all his uncertainty as to whether his magic is going to work or not, there is something faithful, something that he cannot get round, some laws that cannot be broken.

You get the first joy of that discovery, as far as our religious literature goes, right at the beginning of the Book of Genesis, after the flood. Suddenly we hear that as long as the earth endures seed-time and harvest, summer and winter, day and night, shall not cease. Now the idea of God in the Old Testament is often most capricious, most uncertain. Again and again we get the impression that the Jews simply did not know what it was their God wanted them to do.

But nevertheless again and again in the history of man, with all his efforts to evade or frighten his God, to coerce, to persuade, or push Him into doing what He does not want to do, there is continually this discovery that underneath it all there is something or someone who is faithful. As long as the earth endures the natural processes will not fail. With all your magic you cannot stop them. Seed-time and harvest, cold and heat, summer and winter will not cease. And after all the horrible, cruel, fantastic ceremonies of magic, the human sacrifice, the fetish, the ju-ju man, all the blood-stained imbecilities and cruelties of human religion, we draw near to God. By what strange and miry paths have we come home, and from what immeasurable distance has God seen us coming and made haste to meet us!

Through all this tangle of superstition and folly and cruelty and fear, and a desire to exploit the spiritual things and to work the oracle, there dawns on the human mind the realisation that there are some things that cannot be worked, some gods who cannot be bribed, and some laws which cannot be violated; just a few things in the universe that can be trusted. The growing consciousness of that trustworthiness of God is one of the glorious things in the history of religion. It grows and fades, comes and goes. Some religions have had more than others. Some seem hardly to have had any at all. But all have a little, and gradually as the mists begin to clear away we see that God is in fact power and order and love and strength, and when we see that, when we see any part of it, then suddenly comes the possibility of worship.

"Thou hast said, Seek ye my face. Thy face, Lord, will I seek." Religion you can have, but the impulse of worship comes only when God is seen to be worshipful. We may worship false gods; we do; incomplete gods, shall I say.

We may worship God as power, or as beauty, or as wisdom, or as might, but I believe that the history of human progress lies in those moments when humanity suddenly perceives some glory in the nature of God, and worships it with so disinterested and perfect a love that the desire to exploit or make use of Him disappears, and at least for an hour man desires nothing but to see the glory of God. Just as magic is an attempt to exploit God, so worship comes at the moment when the desire to exploit Him vanishes, when the sudden realisation of His beauty, majesty, or power becomes so lovely, so adorable, that the beholder ceases to want to make anything out of it and has nothing more to ask, but his heart goes out to God just because He is so beautiful. "We praise Thee, we bless Thee, we glorify Thee, *we give thanks to Thee for Thy great glory.*" Not for anything Thou hast done or we want Thee to do. We give thanks because Thou art so glorious. And whenever that happens in the world it involves sacrifice. Suppose you are somebody who can secure a good harvest or ensure the fertility of the tribe. If you suddenly come to the realisation that God is law, and you cannot alter His laws, you have got to give up something of your own power, something perhaps even dearer and lovelier than that, the thought that you can help other people. If you were a magician and thought you could produce a good harvest, and you suddenly learned what this great phrase meant, "Seed-time and harvest shall not cease," and you had to stop the "magic" of making a harvest, you would not only give up that bit of power which is dear to you, but you would give up that dear thought that you could serve other people.

Worship must be very disinterested, because whenever that impulse for worship is invoked in humanity by some revelation of the nature of God, it always means that something dear, lovely, or noble as far as it goes, has to be sacrificed. It is not only in your individual life, but it is in the whole history of humanity. Men must claim Him in such disinterested love that they forget what they have to lose. I think there comes just such a moment in our history now. So often when I preach that God is not the source of suffering, people will say to me that I have taken from them the one thing that helped them to suffer. I get letters such as I recently received from a woman who has suffered many things, both in bereavement and in sickness, and she said, "I have always been able to bear these things because I believed they were sent by God. If I have not got even that consolation I cannot bear them." And I suppose there is no one person who has been brought up to think that suffering is the will of God, to whom God is dear and religion true, who has not felt the belief that suffering was the will of God to be a continual inspiration, a source of strength that made it possible for them to suffer, and who feel that I am trying to take away what made their lives tolerable. But we have got to feel such joy at the discovery that God cannot send disease, that God is the Father of light, from Whom cometh every good and perfect gift, in Whom is no variableness neither shadow that is cast by turning, that it will outweigh the personal loss of comfort and consolation. Worship must be disinterested. "Let God be true and every man a liar." There is no other consolation, but again and again humanity has found that consolation enough. I think that cry, "Let God be true and every man a liar" rises from the noblest inspiration of the human heart, that everything else should go so long as God is not less than Himself. That is worship. The joy that goes out with that thought makes your personal loss fall away from you before the glory of the disinterested discovery that God is greater, nobler, more trustworthy, more completely all that the heart of man desires. The response to that has marked the great forward movement of human nature. The great prophets who have moved the world along its path are those who have revealed to us the worshipfulness of God, and if they reveal it to a generation which can forget its own loss, which can cease to desire to exploit God even for its own consolation, can forget it all in the glory of the discovery that God is greater than they knew, such a generation is worthy of a prophet.

THE GOD WITHIN US

"*I have said, Ye are gods; and all of you are children of the most High.*"—Psalm lxxxii, 6.
"*Jesus answered them, Is it not written in your Law, I said, ye are gods?*"—John x, 34.

THE belief that we have in us something of the divine nature is one which has inspired all deeply religious minds, not only of the Christian or Jewish faiths, but of all the great religions of the world. One of the most wonderful hymns in the old Jewish sacred literature is Psalm viii. where the writer, overwhelmed by a sense of the glory of God as he looks at that most majestic of all natural sights, the starry heavens at night, cries: "O Lord, our Governor, how excellent is Thy name in all the world! Thou hast set Thy glory above the heavens. . . . I will consider Thy heavens, even the works of Thy fingers, the moon and the stars, which Thou hast ordained." Then he goes on: "*What is man, that Thou art mindful of him? and the son of man, that Thou so regardest him?* Thou has made him but a little lower than God, and crownest him with glory and worship."

One easily expects the reaction from the spectacle of the majestic starry skies to be a sense of the smallness and impotence of human beings; and when we find the passage going on from the glory of the skies, the moon and the stars, which God has ordained, to the question, "What is man, that Thou art mindful of him?" one almost instinctively expects that the Psalmist will say that in the sight of the stars, man can be of no importance at all. But instead, he goes on to affirm, in the face of the most glorious natural beauty, the majesty of the spirit of man: "Thou hast made him but a little lower than God, and crownest him with glory."

When you compare that with a great many Christian hymns—for the psalm, of course, is pre-Christian—I think you must be struck with the loss that often appears most painfully—the loss of the sense of the dignity of man; so that the translator of this verse dared not translate it as it stood. Perhaps some of you got rather a shock when I read, "Thou hast made him but a little lower than God," because the version you are familiar with says, "Thou hast made him a little lower than the angels." But, as a matter of fact, the word there translated "angels" is the word that is translated "God" wherever else it appears in the Old Testament. The translators' courage seems to have deserted them when they came to the assertion that man was "but a little lower than God," and translated the word "angels."

And when you come to sing hymns in church in which you are expected to call yourself a "worm" and to describe yourself as being composed of dust and ashes, you feel a depressing lack of that self-reverence which Shakespeare said was even a more terrible loss than the loss of humility. To the modern mind there is something very depressing and even insincere, when we think of the majesty of human beings—for after all, humanity is partly divine—in the expression of so profound a sense of abjectness as these phrases contain.

Now I think that as a matter of fact all great religious souls and indeed all religious people do sometimes feel that sense of unspeakable abjectness. When you have done something far more mean and base than you ever thought you could do, something, perhaps, that you always specially despised; or when you come up against some extraordinarily beautiful and lovely character, and you feel what a smudgy, mean little soul you are, there comes over you a sense of unspeakable unworthiness. But I think all the same it is a just instinct that says that this moment of passionate humility is not one which should be set to music and recited in public worship, because to make it permanent and to dwell on it, is to lose in emotion the strength which you should have put into becoming a better person; and very often people spend such a lot of time in feeling that they are worms that they almost become worms by excess of conviction, when really what they are called upon to remember is, "I have said, *Ye are gods, and all of you are the children of the most High.*"

I think the most magnificent expression of penitence that has ever been put into words—that has become a classic of penitent souls—is that great cry of St. Paul's: "The evil that I would not, that I do, and the good that I would I do not. O wretched man that I am! Who shall deliver me from this body of death? I thank my God through Jesus Christ our Lord." But hardly has he expressed the passion of his penitence than he passes to the assertion that he shall be delivered from this body of death by Jesus Christ our Lord, the Word of God made flesh to dwell among us, whose glory we have beheld. Jesus Christ revealed the divine in man; and we are human, we are mankind, and therefore He revealed the divine in us.

It is extraordinary how angry the claim that is made on us when we are told that we are divine makes the average human being. The Pharisees were filled with rage when our Lord defended His claim to be the Son of God, by pointing out to them that in their own writings was the saying, "I have said, Ye are gods, and all of you are the children of the most High." Our reaction to-day to this amazing vocation has been to set Christ far away, and ourselves in a kind of pit of humility: to affirm that He is so different from us that we can expect neither to resemble His character nor to use His powers. That is really what it has come to. Christ used divine powers, and if you say that He is someone quite outside us, separated from us by a chasm which we call His Divinity, then we do not expect to use those powers, and so we have not used them; we think that it is not the will of God that we should use them. How did the Christian Church begin to lose the great powers of Christ over the body and over material things? Perhaps some day some person prayed to be made well, or that someone else might be made well, but had no faith, and his prayer was not answered. But of course, he did not say to himself, "My prayer was not answered because I had no faith"; he said, "It was not answered because it was not the will of God." Falling away from the great claim made by Christ, he ceased to be able to use the powers of Christ. And it has been the same with Christ's moral power, even more important to us to-day.

We do not expect to turn the world upside down, [illegible] do not expect to exercise that divine authority [illegible] that divine love, because we are not divine, [illegible]e only human. Yet we shall not learn to [illegible]iracles, either material or moral, until we [illegible]hold of the idea that there is within us the [illegible]d, that we are all the children of God.

When we have denied ourselves and, so to speak, given ourselves up to God to use, then we shall find that the divine nature does fill us. It sounds like a philosophy, but in fact it is an experience and we all know it in ordinary life. You know that the things you cannot do for people you do not like, you can do and do easily for people when you love them; that the most tiresome little duties become a joy to do when you are doing them for somebody you love.

Everything is transformed by the mere fact that we are doing it for a certain person. Things that you cannot bear in the ordinary way you can bear for them and love to bear: it becomes a joy to you to serve and to bear. What is that but that you have simply put yourself on one side and let the love of God fill you? That is when you can work miracles by love. It is not just a phrase, then, a way of talking, when you speak of "the miracle of a mother's love"; it is a solid fact that because she loves she can do for her children things that no one else in the world could do, not because they are not clever or wise—they may be much cleverer, much wiser—but because they have not the same spirit of God working in them. Very often the mother is not aware that it is God; she may even think it is herself! Or it may be, she thinks her children are so wonderful—she often does think that—when really it is that in dealing with them she herself has been filled with the Spirit of God. It is the same with lovers, and friends, and children for their parents, and patriots for their country, and lovers of humanity for the world; they become filled with the Spirit of God, and when they realise it they work miracles.

The idea of Christ's divine nature being in us creates in the mind of some of you, I think, a theological difficulty; and so I want to point out that the Christ did claim very clearly and definitely to have the Spirit of God. He says, "I and My Father are one." It was because he said that that the Pharisees wanted to stone Him. He always spoke of God as His Father. Only on one occasion in the whole of the Gospels did our Lord speak to God by any other name than Father, and that time is very significant: it was when He believed Himself abandoned on the Cross: "My God, why hast Thou forsaken me?" Even then "My" God; but that is the only instance in all the Gospels where our Lord spoke to God otherwise than as "Father." I am not referring to the times when He spoke *of* God; then He used various terms. But when He spoke *to* God He always said "Father," and the emphasis of His teaching is always on this sense of the Sonship of Himself to God.

The Fatherhood of God, the fact that God is Father, is a vital part of the Christian religion. If that is not true, then Christ was indeed deceived; for above every other religious teacher in the world He emphasised the Fatherhood of God. He did not say, "God is love," as the greatest of His disciples, St. John, did; He said, "God is your Father," and when He spoke to God He said "Father," and when He summed up the relationship of God to man it was in the parable of the Prodigal Son—the son and the Father, the two sons and their Father. He speaks of the Kingdom of God, yet never speaks of a King but always of a Father. Some Christian people have been at pains to point out that although Christ did this He was always careful to maintain a difference between the Fatherhood of God to Himself and the Fatherhood of God to other people. I have read much minute criticism of the phrases in the Gospels to show that Christ always maintained this difference, that He called God "Father," but that He always spoke of Him to the disciples as "your Father," and when He taught them the Lord's Prayer He taught them to begin "Our Father," while He Himself spoke as though He were in a closer union with God, always with some careful, almost literary distinction, between the Fatherhood of God to Himself, and the Fatherhood of God to man. Well, I believed that for a long time, but I have come to the conclusion that that distinction exists only in the minds of those who desire to find it.

As a matter of fact, our Lord did not teach the disciples to pray "Our Father"; it is practically certain that the oldest version of that great Prayer, and the one therefore most likely to be correct, begins like this: "Father"; not "Our Father" but "Father." I suppose the Christian Church was so impressed with the sense that the Fatherhood of God made all men brothers that they instinctively added the word "Our" to remind themselves that they were praying to the One Who is the Father of all. But in fact it seems certain that our Lord gave them the Prayer in this form—"Father"; that is to say, He taught His disciples to address God in precisely the same way that He addressed Him Himself. You remember when He rose from the tomb and was speaking to Mary Magdalene He told her to go to the disciples and tell them, "I have ascended unto my Father and your Father, unto my God and your God."

There are people who will find, even in that, some distinction between the way Christ spoke of God and the way He expected us to speak of God—the distinction between the "my" and the "your." It seems to me that if I had wanted to convey to any human being the fact that God was precisely the same to them as to me, if I had been in the habit of calling God my Father, I would say just this: "He is my Father *and your Father;* my God *and your God.*" I cannot see how our Lord could have more deeply emphasised the fact that they also were the children of God and had in them, because they were His children, His divine nature. Then in the passages that we read for the lessons this evening (John x. 22–38 and xvii.) there is first of all this assertion: "I said, Ye are gods," and then in St. John xvii. there is the phrase "That they may be one, as Thou, Father, art in Me and I in Thee; that they also may be one in us." The phrase occurs several times: "The glory which Thou gavest me I have given them, that they may be one *even as we are one.* I in Thee and Thou in Me, that they may be made perfect in one." Then we go on to St. Paul's great affirmation: "Now I live, yet not I, but Christ liveth in me."

What does this imply, what does it mean, this emphasis on the fact that God is our Father, and that He is our Father in the same way that He is our Lord's Father? Does it mean that Christ was not divine? How swiftly comes that question! How easily we assume that someone is trying to degrade the nature of our Lord, that if we level it must be a levelling down. Do I mean to deny the divinity of Christ? No, I do not. I affirm that God is in us also. It is not the divinity of Christ that I call in question, but I want to affirm the divinity in ordinary men and women, and I am persuaded that Christ Himself sought all His life to recall us to our Father, because it is so hard for us to believe that we really are the children of God.

Is there then no difference between Jesus of

Nazareth and human beings? Try! Try, and find out if there is no difference between Jesus of Nazareth and you! The harder you try the more you will realise the divinity of the Master you are trying to follow; the closer you keep to Him the more you will adore Him; the harder you try to follow Him the more you will worship Him. Why do people puzzle themselves so much about this question? Let them call us to follow Him and we shall find out His divinity! He was the perfect Word of God made flesh; and you and I, what crabbed and ill-written manuscripts are we when we try to reveal the Word of God! Here is the perfect Word of God, conceived before the foundation of the world, without a word misspelt, without a letter ill-written, the perfect revelation of what God is and what He meant man to be. And we are very far away from that, most of us, far enough from the Word of God to realise His divinity. Only, I believe there is no final chasm—that is my point—either between Christ and us, or between God and us.

To the mediæval mind God was one thing and man was another; but to the modern scientific mind all the universe is one, and God, Who is in the universe, is not separated from us by a final chasm. There is no final unbridgeable chasm, because God is everywhere, and therefore in us, even the worst of us. We cannot say, "Here is God and there am I; there is God and here am I";

for God is everywhere and the tiniest flower reveals Him. Take some minute organism dredged up from the bottom of the sea, where no light has ever come, photograph it, and throw it on the screen, and you will see an organism exquisitely beautiful. Does it not tell you something of God? Is there not something of the nature of God in the beautiful? From the highest to the lowest there is God everywhere, and there is no final chasm either between Christ and you, or between you and God Himself, the Father. Whatever you call Christ's nature, there is not a final gulf between us and Him, any more than there is between us and God Himself—who is our Creator and our Father.

What does that imply? It implies that we ought to be able to use the power and to imitate the character of Christ. Do you notice that all the greatest statements of the unity between man and Christ—above all the great prayers, "That they all may be one in us"—come from the Gospel of St. John; and St. John was the great preacher of the divinity of Christ? The other evangelists—I sometimes think that before a modern Synod they would have seemed very unsound about the divinity of Christ! But the author of the Fourth Gospel wrote to prove the divinity of Christ. He does not write about the human Jesus as the other Gospels do. He begins: "In the beginning was the Word, and the Word was with God, and the Word was God"; and every word of his Gospel is designed to prove the divinity of Christ. And yet when I seek to prove the divinity of man I find to my own astonishment that all the greatest examples, the greatest phrases, come out of the Gospel according to St. John. If you dream that I deny the divinity of Christ, I do it out of the words of the very apostle who taught us the divinity of Christ.

Have we not perhaps cut the universe up into too many little hard and fast separate compartments and failed to realise that God is everywhere, and not least in us? Christ looking down on us beheld in us brothers and sisters and, by a lovely extension of that attitude of mind, St. Francis of Assisi, looking down the ranks of creation, found in the beasts and birds his brothers and sisters. For the divine spirit is in all of us, and when we deny it, when we speak of ourselves, not in a moment of passionate penitence, but as a reasoned conviction, as undivine, not having the nature of God in us, what is the result? *We let ourselves off* the high and austere demand of the Christian faith, that we are to be "perfect as God is perfect"; we let ourselves off working the miracles of Christ; we let ourselves off trying to be like Christ.

"Quench not the spirit." The spirit of God is within you. Let us return to the real faith of the Christian religion. Let us not leave it any longer to other teachers to teach us that we are the children of God. What Christ sought to show us, let us not any longer deny. He is the Way, the Truth, and the Life, and we cannot come to the Father except by believing that this is the Way, this is the Truth, and this is the Life; that the life of Christ is in us. "I am the vine, ye are the branches. He that abideth in Me and I in Him the same bringeth forth much fruit. For without Me ye can do nothing. I am come that ye might have life and have it more abundantly."

Let us cease to live a cramped, limited, depressed existence, living, so to speak, on our own capital, on the little bit of light and faith and character that we have; and let us surrender ourselves to the great sweep of divine power. Let God make use of you, and you will find that the saying is true: "I have said, Ye are gods, and all of you—*all of you*—are the children of the most High."

WHAT IS PRAYER?

WHAT is Prayer? Let me offer as answer the first two lines of the hymn we sang just now:—

> Prayer is the soul's sincere desire
> Uttered or unexpressed.

I dare say many of you feel that those two lines are almost platitudinous; gracefully expressed perhaps, but yet a little commonplace, a little trite. "Prayer is the soul's sincere desire"—yes, quite so. I take it for granted that people do think of prayer as "the soul's sincere desire."

To pray is not to say prayers. To pray is not to fall on your knees and to recite a number of collects, or a collection of petitions from the Litany. Prayer is not to gabble things with your lips. We know that persons may say things with their lips that they do not mean in their hearts.

Surely: we all know that! We all realise that prayer is "the soul's sincere desire."

And yet when I speak, for instance, of the deep thirst for knowledge that possessed the scientists of the nineteenth century as "prayer" some of you write to me and say that I am juggling with words! That is why I have to begin by asking—What is Prayer?

Prayer is a request: it is asking for something. There are many people who think it is a very childish idea to think of prayer as asking; but I think that that, if they will forgive me for saying so, *is* juggling with words. To pray *is* to ask. "I pray you" means, I ask you; and prayer is asking; and everybody who prays asks. A person may ask for a bicycle, or he may ask to pass an examination, or he may ask for the Spirit of God; but whatever it is that he may ask for, prayer means asking. It is "the soul's sincere *desire*." If you contend that prayer is rather that act of communion with God when you cease to ask, when you have come so near to the Divine that your will is one with God, and you ask for nothing, I would say that you are confusing the prayer with the answer. That sense of absolute communion with God, which leaves you nothing to ask for, nothing to desire—that is not prayer; that is the answer to prayer; that is the complete and final and infinite answer to your asking. It is joyfully true that most of us sometimes know that perfect union with God in which we cease to ask. It is true that great saints reach it so often and so easily that they may live in a state of contemplation; but that is because their prayer is answered. It remains true that to pray is to ask.

Look back over the history of the world. At one period which we call the Renaissance period the world was thirsting for beauty; it asked for beauty; it sought beauty; it knocked, and the door was opened. And during the last 150 years the world has asked for knowledge, and has received in return a flood of light, an illumination by which our very thought of God has been uplifted and changed. Prayer is "the soul's sincere desire." There are those who may deny that the growth of knowledge was an answer to the prayer of the nineteenth century, that the great works of the Renaissance were an answer to the prayer of the world for beauty. With these people I join issue at once. Prayer is not what you say with your lips. It is the "soul's sincere desire." That is my idea of prayer. Is it Christ's? Yes, I think it is. "*Ask, and it shall be given unto you; seek, and ye shall find; knock, and it shall be opened unto you.*" Even though your Father God knows what you want, yet ask! "Your Heavenly Father knoweth what ye have need of before ye ask Him," says Christ; and yet in the same breath He says, "Ask, and ye shall receive." "After this manner, therefore, pray ye—*Give us this day our daily bread; forgive us our trespasses* as we forgive them that trespass against us; *lead us not into temptation*, but *deliver us from evil*." One petition after another. Even though God knows what you want, yet ask. And that intensity of asking is the sort of prayer that Christ recognises as prayer.

There is something further. Prayer is "the soul's *sincere* desire." "Thou, when thou prayest, be not as the hypocrites are; for they love to pray standing in the synagogues, and at the corners of the streets, that they may be seen of men. Verily I say unto you they have their reward." They pray that they may be seen. That is why they pray; that is what they pray for. And they get the answer. They *are* seen; they *are* praised by men. Let them never say that their prayers are not answered. Let them not say that God did not hear them. They really prayed that they might be seen of men. "Verily I say unto you they *have* their reward." Prayer is "the soul's sincere desire." It may be a desire for something wrong, but yet it is prayer if it is "the soul's sincere desire." What the hypocrite prayed for was the approval of men. I think it is here that many of us find our prayers fail. How often do we know what we prayed for? How unspeakably glib are the prayers of many Christian people! I often judge of what people think of prayer by the way they ask me to pray for them.

People will ask for one's prayers as they will ask for a penny; they will ask you to intercede for them as they might ask a millionaire to write them out a cheque for sixpence. People who would hesitate, perhaps, to trouble me to write a letter, who would hesitate to ask me to give them five pounds, will often ask me to pray for them as though it were a little thing. I do not say that any in this congregation would do so. But have you not shared this experience of mine—that people will ask you for your prayers, as though they were asking for nothing? And yet it is hard to pray sincerely, or even to know what is your sincere desire. It is hard to be sincere. I often think that one of the most enlightening things that our Lord ever said was that question He put to the paralytic man who sat by the side of the Pool of Bethesda year after year, and never had the chance of being healed; and our Lord said to him: "Would'st thou be made whole?" Would'st thou! It is not every paralytic that wants to be made whole. There is such a thing as "enjoying" bad health.

You know the old story of the great saint who went about Italy preaching, and wherever he went the blind saw, the deaf heard, and people were healed of their infirmities, and it was just as in the days when our Lord healed the sick. One day as he was coming into a city the people saw two lame men getting over the ground quicker than you would have thought lame people could. And someone said to them: "But where are you going?" And they replied: "You know that Saint So-and-So is coming, and they say that he heals the lame. If we were healed what would become of our living?" Sometimes it is easier to sit beside the Pool and be supported by the alms of people, than to get up and walk. If you are able to walk then you can work and support yourself. If you are whole you have all the responsibilities of wholeness; you must not "enjoy" the advantages of ill-health any longer. In saying this I know that there are many to whom ill-health, or any kind of physical defect, is a burden very hard to bear; they are only too painfully conscious of the trouble they give to those who love them. God forbid that I should wound the heart or conscience of any such person here; I know too well that burden in my own life.

Yet it is true that there are people who do really enjoy ill-health; who have, perhaps, no other claim on earth to the limelight except the fact that they are never well! You may remember that Max Nordau said there were people who would rather be hanged than not noticed. And so there are people who enjoy ill-health. They may pray with their lips to be made well, but if they will search their hearts they will find that they do not really desire their prayer to be answered. If it were, then they would need to be energetic! Is it not true that sometimes in the recesses of one's mind one does not desire to be made whole?

It is not only so with regard to physical health, but in regard to other things also. You ask, perhaps, for courage. But do you really want to do the things that brave people do? Are you sure that if you saw the whole of the way that courage would make you go—are you absolutely certain that you would really want it? You ask for great gifts. You want to be great. Do you know what it costs to serve the world? If you are, for example, a leader, you will have some day to lead, not only where people do not want to go, but where you do not want to go. Do you really want it at that price? You ask perhaps for humility. I wonder how many people really want it. You know that cynical and witty saying—that "to do good by stealth, and to have it found out by accident is the supreme joy of life." Have you never felt that? You pray for humility. Do you want the fruits of humility? Does not the truth of that cynical and witty saying penetrate into the very recesses of your heart?

Do you really want people not to know how good you are, not to be aware how many good deeds you have to your credit? If you were to realise that to be humble would mean, very likely, that you would succeed in hiding from all the world your good deeds, would you continue to pray for humility? You want all the grace of humility with the advantages of advertisement! Are you really prepared always to pay the price of the thing you ask God for? Is it your soul's *sincere* desire? I sometimes think that if we were really honest in our prayers we should be constrained to ask, not that we might be brave, or humble, or chaste, but that we might wish to be so. We should realise that we do not reach the ear and heart of God with our prayers because He knows we are not asking for what we want. We think we are, but He sees into our hearts. That slow, devastating knowledge of oneself that comes when one strives a little to be honest with oneself only reveals what He has known all the time.

I knew a medical student who prayed that he might pass his examination; and he did not pass it. I remember saying to him:

> I suppose examinations are not always perfect tests, but still, roughly speaking, if you did not pass your examination it was, perhaps, because you were not efficient up to that point. Did you really want to have the credit of knowing what you do not know?

Prayer is the soul's sincere desire. It is the custom nowadays to laugh a little, and I confess that I have laughed with the rest of the world, at that method of healing known as psycho-analysis. Yet the theory that people do not know what their own wishes are is based on something very true. Psychologists have taught us this, at least, and in teaching us this, they have taught us that it is hard for us to know ourselves; that we do sometimes have in the recesses of our minds wishes that we have never admitted, never faced. Do not say you have prayed when you have not sincerely desired. And if you want a test easier to apply than the test of the psychologist or the psycho-analyst, try the test of Jesus Christ. "A certain man heard of a treasure in a field, and with great joy *he sold all that he had* and bought that field. A certain merchant heard of a pearl of great price, and *he sold all the other pearls he had,* and bought that pearl." If your prayer is the prayer of a sincere desire, you will pay the price for it. If you are not prepared to pay the price for it, then it is not a sincere desire.

It is then no longer rational—is it?—to say to me—"What is the use of prayer?" What is the use of prayer? How can you *help* praying if prayer is the soul's sincere desire? "If God knows already that we want these things, why should we pray for them?" someone asks. How can you prevent yourself praying? If this platitude about "sincere desire" is, in fact, not a platitude, but a searching truth, you cannot help praying. Why should a scientist desire truth? Because he does. Why do you desire spiritual things? Because you do. There is no other reason. And that desire is your prayer. That is praying, though you do not always know it. If you will be quite honest with yourself, you may find, for instance, that you dare not ask God to accept you because you do not know what He will do with you; you dare not ask Him to take your life into His hands because you do not know what He is going to use it for; you dare not ask to be shown the way because you have realised that there are ways that are too hard for you to follow.

Instead, then, of going on your knees and glibly asking God to show you the way when you have not the courage to follow it; instead of asking Him to possess your life when you know that He may ask you to do things that you do not really intend to do, be content to ask Him to give you the desire for these things. Do not ask for what you do not really want, and then go about and say that God does not hear your prayers. "Ask, and ye shall receive; seek, and ye shall find; knock, and it shall be opened unto you." That is certain. The hypocrites love to pray standing in the synagogue and at the corners of the streets that they may be seen of men. "Verily I say unto you that they have their reward," says Christ. And so have we all. If we are not prepared to pay the price of the thing we ask for, ours is not really prayer at all. Pray rather that we may be ready to pay the price. Many of us can get as far as that. "Do what lieth in your power, and God will help your good-will." We think we know what we are praying for; too often we do not; but God does. Behind the clamour of our words, behind the clamour of the prayer with which we besiege the throne of God, behind all the noise and din, God hears the voice of our sincere desire, and that prayer He both hears and answers.

WHAT IS FAITH?

"Be it unto thee according to thy faith."
—Matthew ix, 29.

EVERYONE has noticed that our Lord, in urging His disciples to pray, lays great stress on the power of a prayer of faith and on the impotence of a prayer without faith; so that it is rather strange to find that many Christians still believe that the prayer which they send up to God with anguish of spirit is a prayer that ought to receive an answer. Surely it is perfectly clear that if you pray in a great agony of mind you are not praying with faith? If you pray with faith, you pray with absolute certainty and assurance; there is not any room for that agony of mind which probably all of us have felt sometimes, which our Lord Himself felt in the Garden of Gethsemane. The prayer of faith to which our Lord promised such astounding results must necessarily be a prayer of assurance, the prayer to which you *know* that the answer will come; and therefore any kind of agony of mind is impossible. Christ continually told us, not that we must pray very violently or very agonisingly, but that we must pray with faith.

When thinking about what to say to-night, I looked up all the references that our Lord made to the prayer of faith, and it is amazing how great are the promises He made to those who pray with faith and how entirely He puts aside the idea that prayer must be a great agony of mind. You are simply to believe, and the answer is there already. I suppose that that is what a great many twentieth-century people profoundly resent. For people like us, like the majority of us at least, it is exceedingly hard to believe, and we feel that if God had asked anything else we could have given it. But He makes a condition of successful prayer just that one thing which is not within our reach, which we cannot command, and then He says, Unless you have got that, your prayer will not be answered. I suppose to millions of people it has seemed the most arbitrary, unjust and cruel limitation that God could possibly have made. They would say, "If there is anything we could sacrifice we would sacrifice it." Men have sacrificed animals, in shambles; they have even consented to sacrifice one another, if a bullock would not do; they have sacrificed their children; in the last resort, perhaps they would even sacrifice themselves. There is no sacrifice and no effort that they would not make. But faith does not demand an effort, it is beyond the reach of effort; and to ask for that one thing which you cannot give and cannot force yourself to give, seems very cruel to a great many people who pray.

Now I want to call your attention to a side of Christ's teaching which I think is only just beginning to be realised. Our Lord very rarely said, "You must do this," or "You ought to do that." He spoke as the scientist speaks who says: "If you do this, that will follow." Not, *it must* or *shall be so*, but simply, *it is so*. You cannot gather grapes from thistles, not because God dislikes thistles, but because that is the nature of things. You cannot expect fine weather when all the conditions are for bad weather, not because God is vindictive or determined to destroy your flocks or herds or harvests, but because such is the nature of things. If you defy the law of love you will destroy the world in which you live. If you hurt your brother you will hurt yourself. It is not so much, if you look carefully at it, I think, "You *must* not hurt your brother; if you do, God will hurt you." It is simply this: "If you hurt your brother, you will find that you have hurt yourself, for if one member suffer all the body suffers with it." Not, "If you build your house on the sand, God will destroy it in a rage"; but, "Houses built on the sand fall, because sand is not a good foundation."

Now if you will apply that principle to our Lord's teaching about faith, I think you will see that He was not imposing a condition, He was pointing out a fact. He did not say, "God *will not* answer your prayer if you do not believe." He says that belief is *a condition* of effective prayer. If you believe, the thing is there already. That is to say, the power of faith is in the nature of things; it is not that God has arbitrarily decided it shall be so; it is so. The phrase "Christ Scientist" is one of the phrases that twentieth-century people ought to realise and love, for it illuminates twentieth-century Christianity. Christ does not reveal to us a despotic or vindictive God: He simply points out the facts, the great principles that lie in the nature of things. "You cannot hear if you are shouting all the time. You cannot see if you will not open your eyes. You cannot know God if you will not be still." These are facts, these are principles that lie in the very nature of things.

If you are teaching somebody to ride a bicycle or to skate or to swim, they must feel confidence before they can succeed. A person who is learning to skate on the outside edge need not know anything about centripetal or centrifugal forces; he may know nothing about them whatever; but he is trusting in them all the same, and unless he is prepared to yield himself to those forces that govern material things, he cannot skate on the outside edge. It is not any use saying to God, "Let me swim; I will do anything in the world to be able to swim except to take my feet off the ground" because, you see, you cannot swim with your feet on the ground; that simply is not swimming. You may say, "How unjust!" It is not unjust, it is in the nature of things. That is what our Lord is trying to bring home to us when He tells us we must have faith.

What then is faith? I suppose some of you begin instinctively to recite to yourselves some words like these: "The Catholic Faith is this . . . which faith except every man believe faithfully, he cannot be saved." But the idea that faith is belief in a set of doctrines is only very remotely connected (though it is connected) with the sort of faith Christ was asking for when He said that you could not pray effectively unless you believed. It is a very old joke, but it is a terribly true one to many of us, that "faith is believing what you know is not so"; and it is that idea of faith, as consisting in believing, not what is *beyond* your reason, but what is actually *opposed* to your reason, which makes many modern people think that anyone who is a Christian must be mentally deficient. But look at our Lord's words about faith and you will see that, over and over again, His demand for faith is coupled with a demand for understanding: "Do ye not understand? Do ye not perceive? Have ye not understood? Have ye also no understanding?" To Christ faith is based upon understanding. It is not "believing what you know is not so." It is something that *begins* with understanding, that sort of understanding which comes to you in a flash of insight, which you see to be true even though the facts on the surface may seem to go against it.

You remember, some of you, a passage that I read from Professor Soddy on the theory of the Conservation of Energy? He says that the origin of the theory of the conservation of energy was not gathered from heaping together a large number of facts; on the contrary, he says Mr. Balfour[1] was right when he said that "A company promoter who should issue a prospectus based on no better evidence for this tremendous theory than the originators advanced would certainly be in peril of the law"! The gist of Professor Soddy's argument is that

> "the tendencies of scientific belief which, long before there was anything like proof, and often in the teeth of apparent contradiction, have proved fruitful, centre round the idea of conservation. The idea appeals irresistibly to the mind, and then the progress of knowledge confirms it. The progress of knowledge might of course disprove it utterly, but the history of discovery has so far borne out that intuition, and justifies one in respecting deep-seated and universal intuitions as some guide to the inquirer after knowledge."

That is faith, that "deep-seated intuition" which "appeals irresistibly to the mind." Observe, not

[1] *Theism and Humanism:* Gifford Lecture, A. J. Balfour.

to the emotions, not to the heart, but to the *mind.* It is not unreasonable, though it is sometimes, as he says, in the teeth of apparent contradiction; but there is something in our minds so godlike that when we see the truth we recognise it; something so divine that all the shifting shadows of this time-world, all the distorted apparitions, the illusions with which we are surrounded, cannot in the end deceive us. We *know* that the thing is true. Why, the whole advance of science is based on a gigantic act of faith. This is what I mean by faith, this is what I believe our Lord meant by faith.

When the scientist says, as Huxley did fifty or sixty years ago, "If our knowledge were exact enough we could predict the very shimmering of the summer lightning on the horizon," he is making a gigantic assumption: he is assuming that the universe is governed by unalterable law. Could he prove it? Not possibly. Supposing that everything he observed was in accordance with it, yet how little had he observed! How minute was his range of observation, on one little part of this little planet in the vast heavens, part of a universe so vast that we cannot speak of it in imaginable terms of measurement, and yet we do not know whether this one universe is all, or whether, as modern scientists begin to think, there are other universes.

Huxley generalises from his minute little experience, and that of a few scientists before him, and makes the gigantic assumption that we live not in a chaos but in a cosmos, not in a world of senseless anarchy, but in a universe governed by unfailing law. Is there any reason why so gigantic an assumption should be made on grounds so small? Why do scientists accept it? Because it *appeals irresistibly to the mind*. It is true, as Soddy says, that the progress of knowledge might disprove it utterly; it might, but so far it has borne out that intuition. But it *was* an intuition, it *is* an intuition, and it is only because the idea of law, of universal order, of harmony, appeals irresistibly to the sense of truth in that divine thing which we call the human spirit, that science has accepted it. There is no scientist in the world who can prove it—none—but every scientist who accepts it finds himself, within his little sphere, a master of material things.

There is in man an instinct for what is true. How should we ever learn in our little limited life, our bewildering contradictory experience—how should we learn anything at all if it were not that the smallest, the meanest, the least educated, the stupidest of us has yet in him that divine spirit which apprehends the truth? To have faith is to live by that apprehension of truth, which came to you perhaps in a moment of vision, which flashed upon you in some great hour of your life—some sudden perception of the love of God, some glorious conception of the dignity of man, some realisation of human brotherhood, some understanding of the truth of beauty and the beauty of truth. The beauty of truth? In this sordid world, with everyone anxious and broken and poor, the nations full of hate, the world armed to the teeth! Beauty? Truth beauty? Yes, we know it is true; we saw it for a moment; if we saw it only once we can live by it all the rest of our lives.

And so everywhere, in business, in science, in politics, it is the man who has faith who succeeds. Always, at every moment you live, you live by faith. And when it is a great faith, in order, in beauty, in love, in God, or in humanity, then you are finding the faith which makes your prayer irresistible. You have to justify it at every step; you can never finally prove it; but you can and you do justify it by every step that you take forward.

What then is faith? A reasonable faith, a faith that is not superstitious? It is a faith that approves itself to our highest moral and intellectual sense, and which is justified in our experience. Think of those who have had faith in humanity. Talk of believing a thing in the teeth of apparent facts! Why, everyone who believes in human nature has done that, hasn't he? If you read the history of any great movement like—what shall I take?—the movement for the freedom of Italy: if you read the inside history of it—the thing that strikes you most painfully is the treachery, the desertion, the betrayals, the mean and squalid jealousies, the quarrels between the leaders, the jealousies between the rank and file, the misunderstandings, the egotisms, the ambitions, the selfishness. You think, "This is a history of vermin!" It is so foul, so base, so little. But when you get away a little and look at it from a distance you see that Garibaldi and Mazzini and Cavour and the rest were justified in believing so nobly, so gloriously of young Italy. They believed it in the face of facts, but they were right; they had faith and their faith was justified. And you who have faith in some one human being, of whom perhaps everyone else has despaired, are you not the one person in the world who can help that human being?

Have you not yourself felt a thousand times, "If belief in him would only do it, he could be saved; if I can only believe in him I can do it?" If that person had someone to love him, to believe in him, he could still recover himself. If you believe in him, you will make him what you believe him potentially to be. What I speak of in nations is true of individuals too. If you have faith you have power; if you have not, although you may long to help, you cannot.

If you believe in a God of Love you have enough to sustain you. Any one can point to "proofs" that God is not Love, but if you have once understood that only Love can ever create at all, all the blots in the universe will not persuade you that the universe was created by anything else.

Can you believe in a God of law? If you go to heal someone who is sick, what sort of faith is it that you require? It is faith in the lawfulness of things, faith in the unity of God. It is the conviction that God is one from whom cometh every good and perfect gift; it is belief in the great principle that you cannot get sweet and bitter water from the same fountain, that if God is Love He cannot be cruel, and if He is life He cannot also be death. If you have once seen that, seen it, I mean, in the sense that makes it absolutely your own, so that there does not surge up in your doubting mind any more any doubt about the will of God, then you become powerful to heal: but if you are asking for healing while in the same breath you are trying to be resigned to illness, because you do not realise that God is not two but one, then your prayer becomes ineffective.

You feel it yourself, do you not, when you are asking for something? If you feel no certainty that God wants you to have it, how can you pray with faith? It is a necessary condition of effective prayer, not an arbitrary condition imposed by a despotic God. It is obedience to the higher vision; it is to be able to see, beyond the shifting shadows of time, the unalterable purpose of God; it is to be able to understand a little what is meant by love and law and power and wisdom, and all those great sayings of Christ about God. You cannot find the answer unless you believe in the answer, any more than a scientist could find out the law if he did not believe in law; he must believe it before he can find it. You know that great saying of Pascal's: "Thou wouldst never have sought Me if thou hadst not already found Me." If you seek God it is because you feel, whether you admit it or not, that there is a God that answers your prayers. You cannot move humanity unless you believe that it can be moved. You cannot pray to God unless you believe that there is a God.

Have you ever had to deal with a person mentally deranged, who continually desired to be taken home when he was at home all the time? It is one of the most heart-rending things to hear a delirious person ask pitifully to be taken home; and all the while he is there in his home, with his wife and children and everything that he desires. But he cannot believe it! What then can you do for him? There he is, he has what he asks for, but you cannot make him believe it. Nothing is required but that he should believe. Nothing that you can do is any good unless belief is there. And nothing that God Himself can do for you is any good whilst you still doubt whether He is your Father and whether you are at home.

But, you will say, that is just the one thing that you must doubt, the one thing that you cannot believe, and whereas your nurse, your doctor, your wife, cannot make the mentally deranged know that he is at home, God could, if He would, force us to know that we are at home. Beloved, only by destroying you! Only by destroying your own power and freedom! "Be still and know that I am God." "Yes," you say, "but I cannot be still; why cannot God make me still? He *could* make me still!" He could; but it would be the stillness of death. It would be the end of you as a human being, free, and able to see for yourself. And you know, I often think that while we are crying out for God to do that to us, which would in fact mean the stillness of death, we are asking Him to do that which, on the earthly plane, we cannot get a medical man or woman to do.

There are lives which to our human eyes would seem better destroyed, lives so full of agony, so hopelessly broken, that we might say that such a one would be better dead. Would it not be merciful for the doctor just to let him slip away, just not to do for him what would keep him alive? Have you not often heard such remarks? I have. If only we had the mercifulness to do it, it is said, it would be better that such a one should be allowed to die and not suffer any longer.

But you cannot get a doctor to do it—not a man who is really a physician. He may agree with you logically, and admit that such a life is better lost, such a person were better dead; but he cannot let him die. The instinct of the physician is so strong in him that he will fight and fight to keep in life that spark which it would seem merciful to let die out. It is the instinct of the healer that to the end he will fight as though he wrestled with Death itself, to keep alive any broken shattered miserable hopeless human being. And, beloved, God to your soul stands in the same relation. He cannot destroy you, He will not let you destroy yourself. You cry out for the mercy of death. You would rather that God did force you than leave you to fight as you are doing, and to be so lonely, so dark. But He cannot because He loves you too much. More than you love yourself. He loves you, and to the end—yes, and beyond the end—of time He will pursue your soul until you see Him and have faith. Is that mercy? Is it certain? I think it is both mercy and certain. I used to think that since it was true that a soul could turn away from God it was logical to admit that in the end it might for ever turn away, and lose that divine spark that makes it the child of God. But now I see a deeper logic. Our finite resistance is matched against infinite love. Is there any doubt about the issue?

THE POWER OF FAITH

"*I say unto you, What things soever ye desire, when ye pray, believe that ye receive them, and ye shall have them.*"—Mark xi, 24.

YOU will remember that our Lord Himself acted on His own words when He gave thanks to God[1] for having heard His prayer before the prayer had actually been answered. I want to read also some sayings by more recent writers and thinkers on the same point.

Emerson says:

> Man thinks his fate alien because the copula (between person and event) is hidden. But the soul contains the event that shall befall it; for the event is only the actualisation of its thoughts, and what we pray to ourselves for is always granted. The event is the print of your form. It fits you like your skin. . . . . A man will see his character emitted in the events that seem to meet, but which exude from and accompany him. Events expand with the character.

"The soul contains the event that shall befall it." With this compare our Lord's words, "According to your faith be it unto you."

[1] John xi, 41.

Here is another American writer, Orison Swett Marden: "To be ambitious for wealth and yet always expecting to be poor, to be always doubting your ability to get what you long for, is like trying to reach East by travelling West. There is no philosophy which will help a man to succeed when he is always doubting his ability to do so, and thus attracting failure." With this will you compare the passage I read just now: "When Peter saw that the waves were boisterous he was afraid and, beginning to sink, he cried, Lord save me! And immediately Jesus stretched forth His hand and caught him, and said, O thou of little faith, wherefore didst thou doubt?"

Listen to Marden again: "No matter how hard you may work for success, if your thought is saturated with the fear of failure it will kill your efforts, neutralise your endeavours, and make success impossible." "Why could we not cast him out?" said the disciples, and our Lord replied, "Because of your unbelief."

I suppose that our Lord's teaching with regard to our human life is just this: The world contains everything that you require for your human body; there is there everything you can possibly want to make you perfectly happy, and God gives it to you; you have nothing to do but to claim it. If God were not Love, if God were not your Father, it might not be so, but since He made you and knows what you want and loves you, it follows that there is here everything that you want, and all you have to do is to claim it. "Ye have not," He said in amazement, "because ye ask not." And again: "He marvelled at their unbelief." "How is it that ye have no faith? Do ye not understand?" Do not weary God with long prayers, "for your Father knoweth what things ye have need of before ye ask him." It is always the natural assumption that if God is your Father, if He loves you, if He is full of wisdom and power, there must be everything you want in the world and you have only got to claim it.

This is proved by experience. If I read things out of the New Testament you don't believe them; but if I read them out of Baudouin's "Suggestion and Auto-suggestion," or somebody else's modern psychology, or even from some older generation, Emerson or Orison Swett Marden, you say, "Quite true!" Emerson said: "You make your own events; you think these things, so you make them your own." And Marden said: "You want to be rich: if you are always thinking you are going to be poor you will be poor; if you think you are going to be rich, you will be rich." I suppose there are not many people who do not nowadays realise that there is an enormous amount of truth in that. Some people attract success. What they do succeeds. They are confident of it and it happens. They know they are going to be well, they know they are going to succeed, they know they are going to be rich; and they are so. All the trend of modern psychology is to make us realise that this is the effect of wanting something with the absolute conviction that you are going to get it. You sometimes meet people who are perfectly certain you are going to do what they want you to do. Your eyes may be starting from your head in astonishment at what they say you are going to do, but all the same you do it. When other people exclaim, "Why on earth are you doing that?" you think, "Why *am* I doing it?" And the answer is, "Because So-and-so was sure I would do it." That absolute certainty that the things you want to happen are going to happen does to a great extent make them happen.

What are the proofs that this happens on a great scale? As I have reminded you, when the world believed in beauty it got beauty; when it believed in truth it got truth. But it is true of individuals also. You sometimes hear people resentfully say, "That sort of thing always happens to me." They know it "always happens." So it does. Whereas in the case of people who are perfectly certain that things will go right, they go right.

Here there comes in a rather difficult question. There is no difficulty when what you want is something that does nobody any harm, but everybody good. But suppose you are going to exercise the power of faith in regard to a thing that may be somebody else's loss? For instance, to take a very poignant case just now. Suppose you want a job, and somebody else wants it too? For every job going now there are generally hundreds of applicants. Suppose all of them have absolute faith they are going to get it, and yet only one of them will get it? A really conscientious person will hesitate to use power, even if he believes he has it, when he realises that his gain is going to be another person's loss. Even as a logical proposition, how can two people have absolute faith they are going to get a job when only one person *can* get it?

I think that we too often argue from one set of circumstances to a wholly different set of circumstances. I mean this. Some people want to succeed, and they do succeed; they believe they are going to and they do. If all the world—if all this nation even—trusted God; if all the people in this country really believed that God was their Father, and that everything they wanted was here if they would only ask for it, you would have an entirely different state of things to work with. You would find—at least, so I believe—when the whole nation was converted, that there *is* enough, that if this nation would reach out its hands to other nations, if it were composed of people who had absolute faith in God, the entire country and the entire world would be saved by it. There would not *be* unemployment, there would not *be* people in danger of starvation. And when you come down to individual cases, you have to remember that they will not all be using it about one thing because there will be many things; it will not be necessary for anyone to gain at the expense of somebody else's loss; there will be enough work, enough food. The position will be entirely changed. We confuse ourselves by thinking of a difficulty which is concerned with a doubting world and transposing it into a believing world and thinking it would remain the same. It would be absolutely changed.

When you are in difficulty about your own immediate problem in this unchanged world, you will find that if you pray that that which is best may come to you, that that which is the right thing for you to do (it seems to me a better and wiser thing perhaps than to pray for any one job), you will be looked after by God even in these imperfect circumstances. The logical difficulty, I think, disappears, since if we were all faithful, the whole world would be changed; but the practical difficulty for the person who is faithful in an unfaithful world is solved for that individual by the fact that when he commits himself to God, God does take care of him, and his gain will not be at the cost of another's loss. I confess that when I am asking for anything which might conceivably involve loss to another, I am always careful to be sure that what I pray for is simply that God will take care of me and will give me what He Himself deems to be best, with absolute conviction that He does desire me to be happy and well and in work.

But here again another difficulty arises. Perhaps you were struck when I read those passages from Emerson and others, with the tremendous emphasis that is laid on the will and the belief of the human person. It is not stronger really than the emphasis that our Lord also lays on our faith being the operative factor. He says: "According to your faith be it unto you." And again: "Thy faith hath saved thee." And again, when the father of the epileptic boy said to Him, "If thou canst do anything, have compassion on us and help us," Our Lord replied: "If *thou* canst! All things are possible to him that believeth." Again and again He lays emphasis on the fact that the answer to the prayer lies with the individual—with you and with me. He emphasises that just as strongly as Baudouin or any modern psychologist or psychotherapist. The trouble lies in you if you do not succeed; the success is yours if you do. "According to your faith be it unto you." "All things are possible to him that believeth."

And yet there is a difference. If you will read further in our Lord's teaching about faith, you will see that while Emerson and modern psychologists do to a very great extent, not only emphasise the part of the individual, but even speak of power in the individual *alone*, our Lord always assumes the power of God. What His emphasis on the individual really means is just this: God is always desiring you to be well and happy. He always desires you to have enough to eat and drink and wear, and to be free from anxiety; He wants to do everything for you; you have never asked for half He wants to give you: "According to your faith be it unto you." It is not you alone who are doing the whole thing: but if you put yourself in the right attitude to God you succeed.

There is a great difference between that and the view that whatever power there is in faith, it is faith in yourself only. We often speak of everything lying with a certain person, not because he alone can do what is required, but because everyone else who is concerned is already willing. For instance, you might say of Ireland this week: "It lies entirely with the Irish people whether they will have peace or not." You would not mean that literally, for it lies with both countries. It takes two to make a peace. What you mean is that England has now done her part, and therefore the rest lies with Ireland. You do not mean that Ireland does the whole thing by herself. So you say: "God is always wanting you to be happy; it lies with you alone whether you are happy or not." The assumption is that that is so because God is always doing His part.

You sometimes say of a difficult child in a family: "There is everything here to make him happy; his parents are devoted to him, his brothers and sisters love him, he has a beautiful home and everything he can want; it lies entirely with him whether he will be happy or unhappy." There is just a possibility of misunderstanding that. It does not lie with him *alone;* it lies with parents, brothers, sisters, everyone else. But the idea behind it is, they are doing all they can, therefore it now "lies with him." And because God is always doing His part our Lord says it lies with us. We have sometimes understood this to mean that we have to do everything. I think there is a danger in the minds of many people, a fear that the power they have been taught to believe in is really only a power that lies in themselves, and that if they have not got it they can do nothing; that effective prayer is faith in an individual human power which, so far as it leans on any power outside itself, leans on an illusion.

I think one has to judge about the truth of this by the way in which it works—by the power that comes to those to whom faith means putting themselves into communion with something immeasurably greater than themselves, who realise that it is true that it "lies with them" to conquer only because they are so certain that all God's side is perfect. The people who feel that seem to me to be the people who do indeed move the world. The more intellectual process, if I may put it so—I mean the process which is purely scientific—is one which has a more limited scope in influencing human affairs. It is useful because knowledge is always power, and it is a true knowledge up to this point. It is true that it lies with us in this sense to succeed; it lies with us to realise and to use the power of faith. That is true, and because it is true it is a great power. Knowledge is always power. If modern science can teach us something not only of the universe in which we live, but about our own minds, it will give a new power to humanity, and I believe it is doing that; but if your power is wholly intellectual it lacks something of that strength by which some individuals have moved the course of the world; it lacks power to help those who are neither clever—nor rich.

Perhaps that seems strange to some of you. Well, I have a friend who has been undergoing the process known as psycho-analysis for about a year, and I understand she is going on possibly for another four or five years. She has left London and gone to live in another town in order to be nearer to her analyst. I confess I reflected, when I heard that, that psycho-analysis seems to be a religion for the rich. There are not many people who can give four or five years of their life to follow analysts about the country, and though I think there are cases in which this process does help, it certainly does not seem as if it were likely to help effectively a very large number.

And then again. It is not a religion—I call it a religion because to some people it almost is so—a religion which will help very much the simple and the unlearned, and a power which helps all kinds of human beings is a greater power than one which only helps a certain section of the community. A power which enables you to conquer by something that is outside you, your part being to put yourself into communion with that outside power, will help millions, where the intellectual process of analysing your own mind and motives will only help comparatively few. To many of us it seems that our minds, even when they are thoroughly analysed (or even more when thoroughly analysed!) do not make very powerful instruments with which to turn the world upside down; and the sort of power that I am thinking of—the power to which our Lord attached such importance, and which He Himself actually demonstrated by putting it into action—this is the kind of power for which humanity is hungering to-day. It is a great and mighty truth that there is a god within you, or not "a god," but God. All you have to do in order to turn the world upside down is to unite that divine spirit within you with the divine Spirit above. It is a glorious truth that modern psychology is teaching us, that within ourselves lies the key to the problem, within ourselves the power to govern our destinies. We are free, we can, if we choose, command our destinies. But I think it is only half a truth, if it omits the fact that that power within must be in harmony with the Power without, a great and a transcendent Power, if it is going to lift the criminal out of the dust and enable the unlearned to move the world, and to give us a leader whose impact on the world is something made up of the whole of his human spirit, like that of St. Paul, St. John, St. Francis of Assisi, St. Catherine of Siena.

But a man who is really only worshipping himself cannot turn the world out of its course. These men, these Napoleons, break up the surface of the world, agitate it for a moment, do everything and accomplish nothing; but those who worship God disinterestedly are putting their human spirit, which is divine, into touch with triumphant Power incomparably greater than themselves. According to their faith it is to them.

Let me give you a very simple figure which I think may perhaps convey my meaning. If you are trying to swim you must believe that the sea is going to keep you afloat. You must give yourself to the sea. There is the ocean and there are you in it, and I say to you, "According to your faith you will be able to swim!" I know perfectly well that it is literally according to your faith. A person who has just enough confidence in the sea and in himself to give one little hop from the ground will certainly find that the water will lift him but not very much; he will come down again. Persons who have enough confidence really to start swimming but no more, will not swim very far, because their confidence is so very small and they swim with such rapid strokes, and they hold their breath to such an extent, that by and by they collapse; they swim five or six, or twelve or fourteen strokes, but they do not get very far, through lack of confidence.

Persons who know with assurance that the sea will carry them if they do certain things, will swim quite calmly, serenely, happily, and will not mind if the water goes right over them. "Oh," you say, "that person is doing the whole thing!" *He can't do it without the sea!* You might hypnotise people into faith; you might say, "You are now in the ocean; swim off the edge of this precipice" (which is really a cliff). You might make them do it, they might have implicit faith in you, you might hypnotise them into thinking they were swimming; but if they swam off the edge of the cliff they would fall. You can't swim without the sea! I might say to you, "It lies with you whether you swim or not, 'according to your faith be it unto you'"; but if the sea is not there you can't swim. That is exactly what I feel about God. "According to your faith be it unto you." Yes, certainly, if you try to swim in that ocean which is the love of God your faith will be rewarded, and according to your faith it will be to you. In exact proportion to your faith you will find the answer, like a scientific law. There is not one atom of faith you put in God that will not receive its answer. But without God that could not happen. You might have faith but you could not swim unless the sea was there! And because the sea of love is always there, it lies with you whether you will float in it or not. But of course, I always reserve the sense that it could not "lie with you" to do it if there were no such ocean of God's love. A person might easily say, and by saying come to think, that it "lies entirely with them" what they do; but the truth really is that it lies with them only to give themselves to this mighty power.

But may it not be a colossal illusion, this "ocean of God's love?" Admitted that it helps men to live and helps them to succeed—it may be true that the prophets of the world have changed the world's course by this belief in God—but that does not prove that they were right. It may have been a great delusion. It may have been, after all, just themselves and their own power, and their own conviction that enabled them to conquer.

Is that a thing possible to believe? Is the world moved onwards and upwards by a lie? No. Power does not come from believing what is not true. I cannot prove that; it is impossible to prove it. I can no more prove it than the scientist can prove his vast assumption that the world is governed by law. But I maintain it for the same reason that he does, if he will be frank—because it makes an irresistible appeal to the reason. You cannot believe that the world is so irrational, that the universe is so senseless as that power should come to humanity not from knowledge but from a lie. I do not deny that a lie may for a moment agitate the surface of the world, like Napoleon's illusion of belief in force; but even Napoleon before he died said that the thing that struck him most was the inability of the sword to settle anything. Had he lived a few years longer how would that saying have been justified! For every landmark he set up was swept away and the thrones he set up were toppled down. The force of a lie may agitate the world but it does not move it. The contention that power comes from knowledge, not from a lie, is one which "appeals irresistibly to the human mind."

Let me show you how great weight must attach to that appeal. Some of you no doubt know that there are other explanations offered for the great facts which science has revealed to us, than that of universal law. The idea of universal law is, of course, justified by experience, but it is assumed because it appeals to our sense of truth. Now some of you may remember that when religious people were greatly upset by the teaching of Darwinism, and the discovery that the world was not made in six days of twenty-four hours each and so on, a man wrote a book to help people out of their religious difficulty. He saw them everywhere having their faith undermined, and as he was himself a student of natural history whose faith was not at all undermined, he thought he would write a book to show them why they really need not trouble themselves at all. The object of the book was to show that although the world was filled with the evidences of evolution, that the rocks contain fossils and our very bodies contain the vestiges of our humble origin, and all over the face of the earth is written the evidence of change—although, he said, these things cannot be denied, they can be explained. What really happened was that when God decided to make the world (which they believe He did in exactly six days) He put all those things there in order to see what we would make of them! You laugh! Why do you laugh? You cannot *prove* that is not true! But you laugh because such an explanation of creation is repugnant to your reason. You can no more prove that that man was wrong than Darwin could prove he himself was right, but you reject what he says and laugh, and you are right. Such an explanation is inconceivable and irrational, alike to the scientist and the theologian. It cannot be that the architect of the universe should descend to a ridiculous trick like that!

In Milton's *Paradise Lost*, when Adam had a conversation with one of the archangels, he thought it was an excellent opportunity to get to know something about the world in general. So he asked the archangel what the stars were? The archangel replied that it was a thing beyond the human mind, but added that it might be that God put the stars in the heavens in order to amuse himself by listening to men's silly guesses! That makes you laugh again! But how do you know God did not do that? You *know* He did not, and no scientist could convince you more deeply than you are convinced already. You cannot think of God and suppose that it amuses Him to play silly jokes on those human beings whose divine search for truth, whose glorious thirst for knowledge, is one of the most godlike things in us whom He calls His children. You repudiate the idea, because it is repugnant to your whole conception of God if you are a Theist, of Nature if you are a scientist.

I claim that the idea that the power which comes to those who put their spirits in union with a Power outside themselves—with that vast power which in Jesus of Nazareth changed the course of the world—is based on a lie is as repugnant to all that we know of human life and of truth as Goss's suggestion about God putting fossils into the rock to try our faith in the book of Genesis.

Knowledge is power. Do you need me to prove that to you? I could give you a thousand instances; all of you could give them yourselves. You know that knowledge is power; that "knowledge will always trample upon ignorance." Well, if you know that, you know that power cannot be born of a lie; it cannot be born except of Truth.

I sometimes think that if God were less trustworthy, if He were more capricious, if He were sometimes deaf to our prayers, if He sometimes forgot us, we should almost find it more easy to believe in Him; because we ourselves are so capricious, so uncertain, that we find it impossible to realise a God Who is always the same. Because He is always there, always the same, because in fact He is God, we grow so accustomed to Him that we can even say, as someone said to me the other day, "I have done with God"—we who live and move and are sustained by the love of God, may be so unaware of it that we can say, "We have done with God!" "They died for fear," says the author of the Book of Wisdom, "denying that they saw the air *which could of no side be avoided.*" And so we die of fear, denying that we have the power of God which can of no side be avoided. When we have once learned to see that within us and without there surges the mighty power of God; when we can put our faith in it with that simple assurance that we give to the operation of scientific law; those promises of Christ will come true, great as they are and astounding, yet hardly greater, hardly more astounding than those which nineteenth and twentieth century seers and psychologists are making the very commonplaces of our existence.

UNANSWERED PRAYERS

"*Nevertheless not what I will but what Thou wilt.*"—Matthew xxvi, 39.

I SUPPOSE that there is no one in the world who has not sometimes breathed an unanswered prayer—at least a prayer that seemed to be unanswered—and so to-night I want to be very practical in dealing with my subject, because I think that it is a very practical question to most of us. I do not want to dwell very long, though I just refer to it for a moment, on the answer that seems to fail only because the prayer was not sincere. I spoke of that a Sunday or two ago. But I cannot leave it out altogether because so many of one's prayers, if one is really honest about them, are prayers for things we do not really want. You remember our Lord said, "When ye pray, be not as the hypocrites are; for they love to pray standing in the synagogues and at the corners of the streets, that they may be seen by men. Verily I say unto you, They have their reward." I suppose these public pray-ers would have said they were praying for the peace of Jerusalem or for the coming of the Messiah or for all sorts of good and splendid things; but in fact they were praying that they might be seen by men, and they had their reward, their prayers were answered: they were seen. Most of us, if we are honest, will admit that our prayers are very apt to be unreal; that there are certain things that we are taught to pray for, certain spiritual blessings that we do not really want; and when we do not, as we say, "get any answer," it is really because we have not prayed. Words alone do not reach the heart of God; He always sees what is really in our hearts.

I think that is the meaning of that otherwise rather perplexing parable of the importunate widow. Our Lord so often tells us not to pray long prayers, not to use "vain repetitions," not to use a great many words, not to think we shall be heard for our much speaking; and then He tells us the parable of the importunate widow, who apparently *was* heard for her much speaking. The meaning of that parable lies in the sincerity of the desire which made her importunate. It is the kind of importunity that the scientist has who looks for truth. His desire is not a wavering thing, a thing that comes and goes: it is a persistent attitude of mind; and if you desire things in that spirit, with that sincerity and depth, your prayer is heard. A prayer that is simply a passing emotion, the sort of desire which you have to be good when you have just sung a rather sentimental hymn—that is not a real prayer: it is merely an emotion; and the parable of the importunate widow is to teach us to desire and not to faint.

There is some desire behind every prayer. Whenever people pray they want something, if it is only to be "seen of men," or to satisfy their own conscience. That strange habit that some people have of getting up in the middle of the night to say their prayers is probably due to a desire to be very conscientious. They are seized with a sudden fear that they have not said their prayers properly, so they leap out of bed to say them over again. Or they think they ought to get up very early in the morning because what is so disagreeable to them is sure to be agreeable to God, and they satisfy their conscience by doing it. There is some kind of desire behind every prayer, only what I think we fail to understand is that it is that desire that God hears; not the words you say but the desire that is really behind your prayer. Our Lord warned us that the Pharisee has his reward, for he is seen at his prayers. And you realise that if God is really like Jesus Christ, that is characteristic of Him. When anybody asked Christ anything He always went behind the words, to the meaning of the question. If somebody asked Him a question that was stupidly expressed, or that did not express his real meaning, He always went behind the words to answer the meaning. Sometimes it was a good meaning, sometimes it was a bad one; but Christ always answered the meaning rather than the words. So that if you look only on the surface it sometimes seems as if He did not answer at all: but if you look deeper you will see that He did answer the mind of the speaker, though He may not have answered his words. This is a picture of the way in which God answers our prayers. He does not always answer the words, but He answers the meaning behind the words.

Unanswered prayers are responsible for much discouragement among those who pray. For it takes a great and long-continued honesty of mind to be really honest in our prayers. A great deal of our insincerity is simply slipshod. It is not a conscious lie. It is not that we deliberately ask for one thing and mean another. It is that we are so slovenly in our ways of thinking that we do not realise that we are not asking for spiritual power but only—perhaps—to look respectable. Many of us do not realise it, and the harder one tries to be sincere the more conscious one is of the detestably slippery character of one's own mind. The way in which one continually finds that he is not perfectly honest in what he asks shows, I think, that insincerity which is unconscious or half-conscious is very common. But because we do not know we are insincere we think our prayer has not been answered. The Pharisees, for instance, were perhaps praying (in words) for their Messiah; they prayed for the peace of Jerusalem, the glory and the freedom of Israel: but in their hearts they prayed that they might be seen of men; and the Messiah did not come—to them.

You see how easily we may be discouraged? We do not know what we pray for, and therefore we do not know that we have got our answer. That is very discouraging. So that insincerity in prayer is more disastrous even than it seems at first. It is profoundly discouraging to many people to think that they have prayed since they were children for some spiritual virtue which they have never yet achieved. They begin to ask—"What is the use of going on praying? Even when I pray for a thing that is really good, that I know God must want to give me, I do not get it." They do not realise that they never really wanted it, never were prepared to pay the price for it, that in the top of their minds they think they would like it, but in the bottom of their hearts, if they could be honest with themselves, they would see that they did not really want the thing which they asked for *at the cost which such things must demand.* And so, because they do not realise that their prayer is insincere, they suffer from continual discouragement.

When you read a passage like that of Christ in Gethsemane, does it not strike you that the real agony there was that He was torn between two contradictory desires? He wanted to escape, not only I think from death, but perhaps even more from the apparent failure, the desertion, the meanness, the cowardice, the ingratitude with which He was to be surrounded. People sometimes express to me surprise that our Lord should have shrunk so from crucifixion. Remember that so far as we can judge, Jesus of Nazareth at this time was only a little over thirty years of age, and had a perfect physique; that He was filled with the vigour and the strength of an unmatched manhood, and that He was going to die, not on the field of battle, but in cold blood. If He had not shrunk from that I confess I should feel that He was hardly human. But beyond that there was the sense of the anguish of desertion. Peter swore that though all should desert Him yet would he never leave Him; ("Likewise also said they all"), and yet when our Lord took them with Him to Gethsemane, even Peter slept ("Simon, sleepest thou? Couldst thou not watch with me one hour?") at the very moment when the danger was at hand. And then there comes that exquisite touch of gentleness and justice: "The spirit truly is willing, but the flesh is weak." It surely was from that terrible disappointment in the people that He loved, from the ingratitude of those He had served with every hour of His life—the crowd, the multitude, the people—that our Lord shrank; and He could not have had that lovely fineness of nature, that glorious faith in the possibilities of humanity, if He had not also suffered that almost intolerable shrinking from such an exhibition of baseness as He was about to face. "Father, with Thee all things are possible: take this cup from Me. Nevertheless, not what I will but what thou wilt, be done." At the very bottom of Jesus's heart, at the very foundation of His nature, the ruling principle of His whole life was the will of God; and even in the face of grief so terrible, so overwhelming, He still desired above all that the will of God should be done.

Now, God Almighty cannot do things that contradict Himself. That is, I think, where many people misunderstand what omnipotence means. God cannot be both Love and hate. That is not almightiness, that is chaos. God cannot be both one and the same, and many and variable. He cannot change and yet be constant; He cannot contradict Himself. To contradict yourself is not power, it is chaos. God's will for the world was that His purpose should be entirely and perfectly revealed to them as one of love. It was not—do not misunderstand it—it was not that Christ should be crucified. How could a God of Love desire that anyone should be crucified, least of all the noblest being that ever breathed? But His will was that whatever men did to Christ, Christ should not respond by anything but the most perfect love, that He should never use any method than that of love, that if they would not yield to that appeal He should use no other, and therefore if men were bad enough they might even kill Him. This was the will of God, and it is the struggle in the mind of Christ between the two prayers that made His sweat to be like drops of blood falling on the ground—the horror of a lovely and most noble nature at the thing that was come upon Him; and yet even greater than His desire to avoid it, His desire to the end to reveal the love of God.

Here then, is the answer to a prayer that seems unanswered; because what was done by Jesus was the will of God; and that supreme desire which never wavered for an instant during the whole of His life, that He should reveal to humanity what God was—that prayer was answered, and answered by the death of Christ even more than it could have been answered by His life; for, glorious as His life was, it would not have moved the world as it did, without His death. Therefore, the prayer of Christ, like many of your prayers and mine was answered in the deepest sense; that is to say, the thing He wanted above all things was given to Him: and the thing that He asked for, if it were possible to happen with the other, was denied, because it involved a contradiction in terms. And one can see that Christ was aware of the answer to His prayer. Just at the close of that passage, do you not notice the note of triumph? "Sleep on now, and take your rest. It is enough. The hour is come. Behold the Son of Man is betrayed into the hands of sinners." There is something majestic, something triumphant about those words, that make one feel that Christ's prayer was answered, and that He was once more one with His Father.

Let us turn to Christ's other prayers. Have you noticed that He spent a long time in prayer? If you read the Gospels with this thought in your mind you will find over and over again this sort of phrase: "He continued all night in prayer. . . rising up early in the morning He went forth to pray . . . He went up into a mountain apart to pray . . . and when the evening was come He was alone. . . And His disciples came and found Him praying." And yet when our Lord had anything to ask of God, how quickly, how simply He asks! How simply, how briefly He tells us to ask: "Give us this day our daily bread. Forgive us our trespasses." When He was about to work a miracle there was no long striving in prayer, no sense of striving at all. When Lazarus is about to rise from the grave our Lord thanks God for hearing Him before the miracle is worked. There is long communion, but I think very brief petition. Now, are there not many people with whom it is precisely the opposite? Incessant and feverish petition, but very little communion with God? I have been horrified to realise how unlike what one can judge to be the nature of Christ's prayer my own has been during the greater part of my life. The moment one is on one's knees, one begins to offer petitions about this and that and the other, very often about oneself, increasingly often I hope, for other people, but asking, asking, asking, and if one is anxious, asking with more and more feverishness, "besieging the throne of God with prayer," trying to take the kingdom of heaven by violence; and so little able to understand the nature of the God to whom one is praying, so little sure of that communion with God which enables one to listen to what He has to say instead of talking all the time oneself.

I remember hearing a terrible story of men suffering in the war. One of them came home to his people, and his people welcomed him with great joy. They said they had known he would come home safely because they had prayed for him. He said: "Don't talk to me like that, I cannot bear it. It is just chance who comes back and who dies. I prayed for people in the war who have been killed." And then he told his parents how he had once been watching some men who had been retreating under fire. The men ran as fast as they could, until at last they came to a little scrub and managed to get under cover, and there was hope some of them would be saved. Then the scrub caught fire and the men were burned to death. And this young man said that he and his friends had to sit there and watch them. They prayed in agony to God to do something. "We said to God, 'For mercy's sake, do something for these men. If they must die, let them die quickly, let them be put out of their agony; don't leave them there roasting to death.'" But there was no answer: the sky was as brass. And he added "What is the use of telling me that you protected me by your prayers? How could we have been protected when the other men were left to burn to death? We prayed with passion, with madness, and we were not heard."

It is a tragic story, but will anyone suggest that that was a prayer of faith? Can you believe in a God of whom the best that you can ask is, that if He is determined to kill He will at least not do it so cruelly? Do not the very terms of the petition show that these men felt that they were praying to a devil rather than to God? God forbid that anyone should blame them; which of us would not have done the same? How many people could have had faith in the face of such a ghastly catastrophe? But when one takes that as an instance of unanswered prayer, surely it is precisely an instance of the fact that it is not the violence of the prayer but the perfection of the faith that ensures its answer. We make it impossible for one another to believe in a God of Love. We take the world and turn it into a hell, and we call it war, and put soldiers into it, and in spite of their desire to have faith in God, they cannot have it in such surroundings. But—explain it, defend it, as you will—it remains a fact that such a prayer is not a prayer of faith. The prayer of faith is that perfectly calm and simple petition, "Give us this day our daily bread. Forgive us our trespasses as we forgive them that trespass against us:" and the exact opposite of the effective prayer is the prayer that most of us utter whenever we really need something very greatly.

Many of you have been reading lately Baudouin's "Suggestion and Auto-suggestion," and I dare say many of you remember with peculiar poignancy the chapter called "The Law of Reversed Effort." It is a chapter which discusses the fact that, with some people, merely being *determined* to get better has a precisely opposite effect to that which they intend and hope. They are told that they will get better if they will believe that they are going to get better, and they translate this, just as we have translated the prayer of faith, into a frantic effort to get better by an act of will; and the harder they try to get better the worse they get. A simple instance and one familiar to many is the attempt to go to sleep. Baudouin, and his master, Coué, will tell you that if, when you get into bed, you are sure you will go to sleep, you will go to sleep. But imagine yourself in bed and saying "I *will* go to sleep, I *will* go to sleep." At the end of an hour you are wider awake than ever you were in your life, and in the morning, after having spent a sleepless night, you say, "This suggestion business is not any good to me." I heard Coué lecturing the other day, and he said his method would work in the case of everyone who is not an idiot.

It does not work with me, so I said nothing! But I know perfectly well why it "won't work with me;" it is because I cannot keep my will out of it. Coué says that when you pit your imagination against your will, imagination wins every time, the will is always defeated. If you really think you are going to sleep, to sleep you go; but if you *determine* to go to sleep you won't go to sleep. Everyone here probably knows that by experience.

Does not this put into modern scientific language what Jesus of Nazareth told us two thousand years ago? It is not the effort of your will that will ensure the answer to your prayer; it is the perfection of your faith; and just as Coué or Baudouin will tell you to-day that by "the law of reversed effort" the harder you try the less you will succeed, and that what you have to do is not to try at all, but simply to believe, so our Lord told us two thousand years ago not to work ourselves into a fever, not to be anxious, not to be troubled, but to believe that our heavenly Father knows what we want, and the moment we believe it, everything is there for us. Is it not true? When you are obsessed with anxiety, when you really doubt in your heart whether God does care enough for you to give you "good things," and you try harder and harder to believe, your desire goes further and further from you; and you say "My prayer is not answered," when what you really should say is, "I have never yet prayed *with faith* for anything I wanted."

Now may I say something to comfort those who find this sort of faith so hard? I do not believe there is a person alive to whom it is harder than it is to me, and if I have the feeling that I am an idiot when I hear Coué lecturing, so when I read the Gospel I have the feeling that I am a very unfaithful servant; and so I want to say something if I may, of practical comfort to those who also find faith very difficult. Try to spend longer in realising what God is like, and less in asking Him for things. You see, if you really accept the fact that God is Love, all-powerful and all-wise, the petition will come at the end of your prayer with the simplicity of a child asking its father for something. "Your heavenly Father knoweth that ye have need of all these things." But most of us do not realise that, and even when we are convinced of it intellectually it does not get that kind of hold on us that makes it perfectly simple to say, "Give us this day our daily bread."

Do not, then, fall on your knees and begin at once clamouring for something that you are terribly anxious to get. Remember first of all to Whom you are addressing your prayer; try to realise that it is your Father to whom you speak, and that He is able to give you what you want, and that He is trying to give it to you, so that there is nothing left to you but just to take it. It takes a little time to do this; you find yourself continually breaking off to remember how anxious you are. Realise instead that the faith that our Lord asks for is not the thing that works the miracle: it is God who works the miracle, it is God who has all these things in His hands. The faith that He asks for is only the channel through which God gives you what you need: but He is always trying to give it to you. Do you see? Some of you write to me and say, "What is the sense of a God who won't give me something that He knows is good for me until I ask for it? He knows all the time I want it and ought to have it, and yet He won't give it to me until I pray to Him in the right kind of way!"

This idea that God is a reluctant kind of person Who has to be pushed into giving you something, Who has to be worried into doing something that He would never do if you had not importuned Him to do it, though He knew all the time that you wanted it, is the real difficulty, is it not? Realise that God is there, trying to give you all you want, and that the act of faith He asks is simply that you should see it and take it, like that person of whom I spoke last Sunday who asks to be taken home when all the time he *is* at home, and all that is necessary is for him to *see* that he is at home. It is like a child who asks for food but will not open its mouth to receive it. Would anyone say, "What a cruel parent?" It is the child who is refusing the food! Do you see? Always the thing is there, always God is asking you to receive more than your heart can imagine of beauty and joy and health. All He asks of you is that you should be willing to receive it. Understand that He is there asking you to take it. Only because He asks you all the time and never fails you, never once has failed in anything, you do not even realise that He is there!

If you would spend more time in realising how intimately, tenderly human (and because human therefore divine) is the relation of God to us, you would be able to make that act of faith. Do you realise that when our Lord said, "Abba, Father," He was using a word which should be translated by something even more endearing, more childlike, than the word Father? As somebody said to me once, it is more like "Daddy" than Father—like a pet name; and the evangelist has kept the very word itself, the translators also have kept it, as though to bring home to us the exquisite familiarity of our approach to God. "Abba, Father." "Your Father knoweth that ye have need of all these things." When we see that, request is so simple, so easy, so swiftly answered, that we can thank God for having received it before it has come. How are we to get that attitude of mind? May I suggest one thing that has helped me tremendously? The world to us is much greater and more wonderful than it was to previous generations. Some of you perhaps are reading Professor Thomson's book as it comes out, "The Outlines of Science." You will have read something of the modern theory about other universes than our own, something which conveys to you a sense of the immensity of creation, more vast, more majestic, more sublime than any other age could have known, something of which it is true to say that the imagination has not grasped it, and yet which moves the imagination to a sense of awe and wonder. This is the power of God; behind this lies the mind of God. You, with your little difficulty, are in the hands of One to Whom this has been possible.

Use what help you can get from modern science, for it is much. In the world you have enough to hinder you, because it is partly the immensity of our problems, partly the complexity of our minds, that makes faith so hard to twentieth-century people. It is much harder for us to have a simple faith than it was to people a thousand or two thousand years ago. But if we have got that greater difficulty we have also a greater sense of the power of God. Conceive the mind that has created this! How can anyone look at the solar system alone and think of it all as being without a mind? But if you grant a mind behind it, what a mind! If you grant a power behind it, what a power! That space beyond space and universe beyond universe, greater than our imagination can conceive! And your little difficulty—how easily He can solve it!

But then, is He willing? Some people, I find, are so overwhelmed by the vastness of creation that they ask, "To what purpose do I pray to such a God? I ask God to find me a job here in London—a God whose mind conceived the universe of universes!" Look then at the other end of the scale; look at the beauty of little things. "Consider the lilies how they grow:" "Are not two sparrows sold for a farthing? Not one of them shall fall to the ground without your Father." Imagine the construction of a lily, the exquisite care of that tenderness and love that is suggested by the beauty of a butterfly's wing, or the beauty of those things which the microscope alone can reveal to us. When you have lost yourself in the power and wisdom of the Creator, remember that all that power and all that wisdom went to the making of every individual; so that not only is your problem easy for God to solve, but He cares enough to solve it. He made you as you are, unlike every other human being. How can you lose the sense of His love?

Do not be troubled that your faith is not perfect. When I say that faith becomes easier, you think, perhaps—"Yes, for a moment; but we are told that we should have perfect faith." True, but "*according* to your faith" it is to you. There is not one iota of faith that you have ever put in God, in man, in the universe, that has not received its legitimate and exact response. Whatever it is that you pray for, the mere fact that you pray shows that you have some little faith in an unseen power, otherwise would you waste your time in prayer? Trust God a little. If you cannot pray with the faith of Jesus of Nazareth, or St. Francis of Assisi, or St. Joan of Arc, never mind; the mere fact that you are praying shows that somewhere in your heart you have a faint belief in the power and love and wisdom of God. To that little faith, that faint shadowy belief, the reply is as certain, as scientifically certain, as the reply to the mighty faith of Jesus of Nazareth; and this is as encouraging to us as the insincere prayer with its no-answer is discouraging. For if some of us have any faith at all, it is because we have discovered on examining ourselves honestly that even to the faintest little dawn of belief in a God of Love Who hears, there has been an answer.

I sometimes feel, do you know, that those of us who pray the worst and who have least faith, can use our very infirmity to help others. If you had great faith nothing would be impossible; but if you have only a little faith, if in your prayer there is much doubt and little confidence, the fact that that little faith has received an answer is almost overwhelming in its glory. In looking back, you ask yourself if you even believed at all, so many doubts came, and so much anxiety was there; so little of the glad confidence of a child speaking to its father; and yet in accordance with your faith it was to you. You could not believe perhaps that God would heal you on the spot, but you had a faint kind of faith that after all He would look after you, and He has.

You did not believe in some great and earth-shaking miracle, but it did just seem to you that since He said that you had to use your talents He must have meant that you should find an opportunity for using them; and that has happened. Over and over again in my experience, I have known faith so weak answered in a way so unexpected, that the pray-ers did not realise that it was the answer to their prayers; they thought it was a coincidence, chance, and yet if they look back they see that it was God's answer to a little faith. They perhaps prayed a great prayer; perhaps they prayed for the eternal stars; but their faith was very little, and they got a little answer. Yet they did get what their faith could reach to; and, looking back on life and seeing that which has happened, it becomes possible for them to dream of the day when they too shall have the faith which moves mountains.

PRAYER FOR OTHERS

"*I have prayed for Thee.*"—Luke xxii, 32.

I HAVE often been struck by the small number of people who believe in intercession at all. Even those who think they have, often show that it is not real faith by the fact that they never go to an Intercession Service. This has been brought home to me and some of my colleagues very much during the last few weeks. We have been preaching three-days' missions in several places. Everyone who helps in the crusade agrees that we must pray for the crusade beforehand, and while it is going on they all agree to do so, but so far as I can gather hardly anybody ever dreams of doing it. When we say, "We attach very great importance to your prayers," they say, "Oh, yes," in a very perfunctory sort of way, but so far as I can discover very few people believe in intercessory prayer to the extent of taking any part in it! The lack of power among Christian people to-day is due to their disuse of prayer. It is the most powerful force that exists.

I want to convince some of you to-night that

it is really worth while to give time to praying for other people. It is true that our Lord has only once, so far as I can find, told us to pray for others. It is in the Sermon on the Mount, where He says, "Pray for them which despitefully use you and persecute you." But I suppose if He urges us to pray for our enemies it is because He takes it for granted that we shall pray for our friends! Elsewhere He tells different people, His disciples especially, that He has been praying for them, and one of the most striking instances is in St. Luke (xxii, 32) when He tells St. Peter He had prayed for him—"I have prayed for thee that thy faith fail not."

Many of you, I know, ask yourselves what is the use of praying for other people. Is it possible that God should be so cruel and so unjust as not to help a certain person because people did not pray for him? That seems an extraordinarily unjust thing to do. Because a certain unfortunate person had no one to pray for him therefore God would not do what is necessary for his safety! I want to remind you that although it may be true—I am not going to discuss the point to-night—that it is very unjust and cruel of God to give us the power of helping one another (which of course also implies the power of withholding that help) still it is not more unjust or more unreasonable in the case of prayer than it is in the case of any other kind of help. I mean this: if you think it is not necessary for you to be kind to people, or to give them food when they are hungry; that it is not necessary for parents to sacrifice themselves for their children because surely God will look after them without assistance; then it is unreasonable also to pray for them. But if one kind of help is rational then the other kind is so too. It is only our curious habit of separating spiritual from material things that misleads us.

Hardly anybody ever says to me, "It is unjust that babies should flourish when their parents look after them; surely God could look after them without their parents?" Yet the help that the parent gives (and could also withhold) is just as arbitrary, just as capricious if you like, as a prayer. It is on exactly the same level. I admit that if you like to argue that God should not have made us dependent on one another, you have an arguable case; I want to speak about that at another time. But if you accept the fact that you *are* dependent on other people—a fact which no human being can deny—it is not sensible to cut off this one particular point of dependence and say, "People ought not to be dependent on one another's prayers." We are dependent on one another for food and clothes; there is not a thing that we wear or eat that does not come to us through human hands; that we are dependent on one another for these things is a fact that stares us in the face.

But we are also dependent on one another for

spiritual things; for our very knowledge of God we are dependent on others; it is what the prophets have told us and the saints have shown us; it is the love of our parents, our children and our friends that teaches us something of God. Therefore to say, "We ought not to depend on each other's prayers" is unreasonable. There is no sense in saying that God "ought not to require" this particular help. Human beings need all kinds of help from one another, and to pray for others is only one of the innumerable ways in which humanity is knit together.

Then this kind of prayer which we call intercession—praying for others—is really a test case for prayer. It is easy to think that if you pray for yourself you have really only suggested to yourself various things you would like to happen, which therefore are quite likely to happen. There are some Christians who would even preach that this is all that prayer is. There is some old tag—I cannot remember the exact words—which runs something like this: "Who rises from his prayer a better man, his prayer is answered." If what you were praying for was that your friend should be a better man, you do not feel very well answered if you are merely a better man yourself! And the saying that prayer should not be asking—only communion with God—is not of much assistance when you come to pray for other people. If you wish to pray for somebody else, to find that your prayer has left you a more spiritual person is not really very satisfactory. Therefore to pray for others is the crucial test of the power of prayer.

So I ask myself, What does really happen when I pray for other people? A number of things happen. First of all, I have frequently found that when I pray for other people I discover something that I can do for them. When you pray for another person, your mind is full of that person in a sense that means love. You do not pray for them unless you love them. I should even be inclined to say it is no use praying for them unless you have some feeling for them which could come under the term love, and I think that is why many of our intercessory prayers seem to be unanswered. People ask one in such an appallingly glib fashion to pray for whole lists of people. It takes a very great saint to be able to love, with any reality at all, a list of people of whom he knows absolutely nothing but that somebody wants him to pray for them. If you want to pray for people I think it is right and wise that you should ask to know as much about them as you can. Sometimes it may be that you cannot know; it may be a betrayal of confidence to know; but I am certain intercession is made much more real if you know enough about the person for your human imagination to be able to dwell on him with something like sympathy; and sympathy is love.

Merely reciting a list of names does not get

anywhere. You might as well write them on a wheel and roll it, like a praying wheel. That has no power. If you recite a list of names and nothing happens, I tell you plainly it is because nothing could happen. There is no power there. Intercession is a great gift. It is that kind of gift which makes a priest—that power of loving human beings so much that even a name becomes real. But this means long practice in intercession, and it means a capacity for being moved to compassion by human needs, so that one can feel positive love for everyone who wants one's prayers. I notice that our Lord, when He was about to work a miracle, was "moved to compassion," and *then* He said, "Stretch out your hand" or "Arise and walk." He was "moved to compassion" when He saw the multitudes hungry, and then He fed them. Intercession must be real. When you are moved to compassion your prayer goes up to God with power.

Then again, when you think of people in this human kind of way, because they are to you real persons in real distress, it is extraordinary how often, while you are praying, a way to help them occurs to you. Get rid of the idea that so many people have when they pray the Lord's Prayer, that "Thy will be done" means that God is to do it, and instead get hold of what (I am persuaded) was Christ's idea, "Here I stand ready to do it." You will then see how natural it is that when you pray for another person the answer very often is the discovery by you yourself of some way in which you can help them. That has happened to me again and again when I had not the smallest idea that there was any conceivable way in which I could possibly help. When I realised that very likely it was I who was going to be the person to help—when I said, "Thy will be done for this person, and here I stand ready, if possible, to do it"—then again and again I have found something I could do. When you pray for others you are thinking of them, you have their circumstances in your mind, their difficulty or their want and, thinking of it in that way, it frequently flashes across your mind that there is some way in which you can serve them. That is one answer.

But suppose there is no way in which you can serve them, still you, when you pray for them, are making yourself a channel for the power of God. God seeks to enter into the universe everywhere. He seeks to possess you and me and the person for whom we pray, and when He is able to find someone who will open the door for Him, who will make a way for Him, He comes. We all have the power in a sense to shut Him out. You can make yourself a non-conductor so that God cannot get through you into the world. When I look at the starry night, I always think of that as a revelation of God; it is so beautiful that it is divine. But it does not stop there. The beauty of it lifts my heart to God, and He comes through it to the world. And so with a human being. If there is a person filled with love—and as St. John said, that is the same as being filled with God—God comes there, into the world. That is why every saint makes God possible to the rest of the world! He has become a channel through which God enters into the world again to possess it.

And when you pray, especially when you pray for others, it is good, I think, consciously and deliberately to offer yourself as that point of contact, as that channel; empty yourself of yourself and offer yourself to God as a means. You do not know how He will use you. I think one of the strangest instances of that was a friend of mine who once said to me such a lovely thing that it has helped me all my life. It was such a help to me that when I saw people in the same sort of distress I used to say it to them. And one time I reminded my friend of it. She exclaimed, "What a perfectly lovely thing to say! Who said it?" I said, "Why, you did!" "Oh no," she said, "it is a beautiful thing to say, but I never said it!" She was filled with love and with the spirit of God, and it reached me through her. She had not remembered what she said, yet it had put a light into my life that has never gone out. And when you pray for other people you cannot guess in what way you are going to be used by God as His channel; only offer yourself continually for that power to be poured through you. That is the way in which great causes are helped. You cannot reach the leaders, perhaps, and yet by offering yourself as a channel for the will of God you help to purify the atmosphere, to create a right public opinion. You help that person by an invisible power.

And I believe you can direct that power. You offer yourself to God and He possesses you and passes on into the world beyond. You can direct that power to the person you desire. Here I get beyond anything I can possibly prove except by experience. I can only say to you, "O taste and see how gracious the Lord is." This is a real power, and because it is real you can direct it to people; and you will see that it has made a difference. But what kind of difference? Here we come across another difficulty. Suppose I pray that somebody shall do something which I think they ought to do. Have I the power to make them do it whether they want to or not? No, I do not think we can compel them, and I think that is why sometimes it takes so much more patience and love to pray for other people than for oneself. Look at that case of St. Peter. Our Lord says He had prayed for St. Peter, and that He was sure he would recover himself and help other people. Well, I do not doubt that our Lord prayed that St. Peter should not fail. That would be the obvious thing to do, wouldn't it? And His prayer was not answered in that respect. St. Peter did fail, and our Lord evidently knew he was going to. Prayer for others works just as the love of God works. It never coerces anyone.

Many people seem to me to wish that God should coerce them. They say God ought to *make* us do this, that, and the other. But He does not, because love cannot do that. When shall we realise that love can only work after the laws of its own being? It is no use asking God to be love and to work as though He were force. God is love, and love can only work as love. Take any great force in the material world; you will realise at once that it is no use treating gas as though it were electricity or electricity as though it were steam. Each has a great power, but each works after the law of its own nature: and love also works after the law of its own nature, and it cannot coerce. That is what it does not do.

You can coerce people just as much spiritually as physically. I have known people who exercised a kind of spiritual bullying over everybody. There are people who say they are going to commit suicide, or that you will make them ill, or something of that kind, if you do not do what they want. That is spiritual bullying. I expect many of you have suffered from it. It is very often done by religious people. They say you will bring their grey hairs in sorrow to the grave if you do not go to their particular kind of church. That is not love; that is spiritual bullying. You can use a spiritual power as brutally as any material one, and people constantly urge that God, because He is spiritual, should use spiritual coercion; but He will not. Love cannot act in that way. But that is not the same as to say that God does not help you, that the love of God does not sustain you at every turn. He is like a parent who gives his child freedom, but is always helping his child all the same. He draws off when the child is old enough to decide for himself, even though he knows he may decide wrongly. But his love is always there. Even if the child goes wrong he knows he will come back some day. Love will always draw him back at last. And that is how the love of God works in the world, and that is how intercessory prayer works. It does not coerce. God will not take your human freedom and force it into His shape, and you cannot take the human freedom of your friends and force them to be what you like. But when you pray for them you direct towards them the power and the love of God in a way which I cannot explain, for after all, who can explain the operation even of human thought?

Those who are teaching us most about it to-day know best how deep is the ultimate mystery, the impossibility of saying why (for example) suggestion makes you better, or how it affects the world, and yet they have the absolute knowledge that it does so. And so in prayer for others. I think when many people pray for one, and do it with great love, it does become a sensible power. I have felt it so again and again. That is why I feel so deeply that if only people would believe in it, would believe in it enough to try it, there would rise in our hearts a sense of power, not only to be ourselves better, but to make the world better, so that nothing should seem impossible.

If there is anyone whose difficulty seems to you insoluble, pray for him. You may find a way of helping him, but if you do not, if you never know how to help him, if it is nothing that you humanly can touch at all, you are still surrounding him by a power to which in the end he will respond, not by the violation of his personality, but as people naturally and inevitably respond at first or at last to love.

This is absolutely certain. It is so certain that I would ask those to try it who have only a very little faith in it, and believe that that little faith will meet its response. We owe a great debt to science for the knowledge that power must always work according to its own laws; that you cannot evade it, and that you can always rely on it. So is it with the power of prayer; it is not capricious; it is in accordance with your faith. Whatever degree of faith you have, so will be the answer.

And I appeal to you with the deepest conviction to pray even for such remote and difficult things as the problems of Central Europe, of India and

Egypt, for the whole suffering of the whole world, with the absolute certainty that in accordance with the faith of your prayer it will be given both to you and to them.

TO WHOM DO WE PRAY?

"*When ye pray, say 'Father.'*"[1]—Luke xi, 2.

IT is not possible to get any clear idea of what prayer ought to be until we have discovered to whom we address our prayers, and people sometimes think very strange things about the God to whom they pray. They have thought that He was the kind of person who would like numbers of animals to be killed in His honour; they have thought He might like human beings killed in His honour. Some people have even imagined that He wanted them to kill their own children in His honour. Many people said that He demanded the slaughter of eight or nine millions of young men during the War. Some people have supposed that He insisted on this gigantic sacrifice because a certain number of people in different parts of Britain played football on Sunday. Others that it was because the Welsh Church was disendowed. They worshipped a God who brought havoc on France, Belgium, Russia, Germany, because we

[1] This is believed to be the oldest form—not "Our Father" but "Father."

English disestablished the Welsh Church! In a book[1] of Dr. Dearmer's is described the effect that would be created on the mind of a man who should address his prayers either to a crocodile or to a god who had the mind of a crocodile. Mr. Harold Anson (in "Concerning Prayer" describes some of the strangely-conceived gods to whom people have made their prayers.

> One will like gold; another will demand blood; while the favour of others will most easily be secured with ivory, apes, and peacocks. One will crave the dead bodies of his enemies; another will prefer the heads of his nearest relations.

He reminds us that throughout, not only what we are pleased to call heathen religion, but throughout the Bible, even, this view of God recurs. In the Old Testament he believes the Jews "rid themselves in a very considerable measure of the degrading associations which had surrounded the gods of old" but indeed we find that it is not only in the Old Testament nor among the Jews that so strange a god is worshipped, and Mr. Anson gives us extracts from a book of more modern times written by St. Ignatius.

> Consider the anger of God avenging this first sin [of Adam] on all the descendants of the first sinner: pestilence, war, famine, desolation of the earth; so

[1] "False Gods."

many disasters, so many violent deaths, so many tears shed, so many crimes committed, so many children for ever deprived of the sight of God, so many souls cast into hell. What consequences and what chastisements for one single sin! . . . One single sin, committed before the Incarnation, before he had experienced the justice of God; above all, a sin which he expiated by nine hundred years of penitence. . . . There is, perhaps, in the depths of hell a soul that God has eternally condemned for such or such a mortal sin committed one single time. . . . Ask yourself what this God is who punishes a single mortal sin in this manner.

Well, I ask myself how could anyone worship such a God? And yet I realise that to generations as far removed from us as we are from St. Ignatius many of our ideas of God will perhaps appear not less terrible and strange than the ideas that I have just described to you from pre-Christian, from Old Testament, and from more modern times.

But the knowledge that other people will turn with scorn from the shallowness, the meanness, the sordidness of our ideas, should only spur us to make the utmost effort to discover what God is really like; for we have not got very far yet. People think of Him, they have been taught to think of Him, as a God who delights in war; Who even in war is strangely capricious and unjust. They say that "God always takes the best," when some brilliant young life, full of promise, is extinguished by a German shell. We have decided to settle our international disputes by a method which is hideously impartial as between good and bad; but yet has a slight bias against the good because the good are on the whole likely to take the posts of greatest danger: and then we ask ourselves why it is that *God* "always takes the best!" Human life is vitally lowered and sapped by the conditions of war, and the conditions of what we call "peace" and consequently a pest like influenza takes a virulent form and becomes mortal; and again we ask ourselves why it is God so often takes the best! Someone dies who does not think of himself or herself and therefore is likely to be in the way of a danger—which we have caused—and we say how capricious is God, Who so often takes away the best!

When, therefore, we pray, we are apt to spend a great deal of time in telling God what He had better do, feeling by no means sure either of His wisdom or His power; we entreat Him to do it and then we waste a good deal of strength in being anxious for fear that He will not. We have no assurance that He wants to do the best for us nor have we any conviction that He knows what the best is, and the faith which brings the answer to prayer becomes for these reasons a demand upon us both unreasonable and cruel. If God is really so capricious and irrational, for Him to ask us to have faith in prayer is most unreasonable, most cruel. It is not possible to have great faith in such a God.

To whom do we pray? Many people pray to one who seems to me more diabolical than divine. Their prayers go into the void, for this being whom they imagine is not there. There is no such being, there is no devil. Evil is the absence of God and those who pray to evil and caprice send forth their prayer into the void.

Do you perhaps pray to yourself? Well, that is something. You have a certain amount of power. There is a divine spirit in you and you can achieve something by your soul's sincere desire: but the conquering power of a great faith is almighty in power and is only possible in proportion as we know and truly worship the God to whom we pray. I think that is what our Lord meant when He said, "Ask in My Name," and—"When ye pray, say 'Father.'" If we who are evil and stupid know how to give good gifts to our children, how much more should our Father that is in Heaven know and give them! Should we give them something lovely? That is what God is like: that is what He desires to do.

This is, I think, why we should continually seek to know more and more about God. Now we see through a glass very darkly, but some day, face to face. Now we know a little, but at last shall know even as we are known; and on the degree of our knowledge our faith depends. The faith which is required to make our prayer effective depends on knowledge. It is not knowledge but it depends on knowledge. The difference between faith and superstition is precisely this, that faith depends on knowledge and superstition on ignorance. If you are going to make a leap you take a run; but if you run in the wrong direction the further you jump the further you are from your goal. Faith is a venture indeed. But its basis is reason. Reason as far as you can. Know all you may. Be honest with your God and with your reason. Then and only then, take the leap which we call Faith. If you do not take the trouble, with the most single-minded and austere determination, to find the right direction, how can you hope to reach the goal? You do not know where you are going! Shut your eyes to knowledge, refuse the light as religious people have a hundred times refused it, and then your faith becomes superstition, and the god you pray to is not there. But if with all your moral sense and intellectual power you seek to know God, your prayer will ever surely find Him. The one is power, it is faith. The other is weakness, because it is a lie.

To believe what is not true is to become weak and powerless. Let me take an extreme example. If a man believes that he is God, he believes a lie. There are people who believe it. It is not an uncommon delusion among the insane. But such a belief does not bring power and freedom. On the contrary, it makes the deluded believer useless and helpless, because though he believes with the utmost conviction, what he believes is a lie.

But if you believe that there is a divine spirit within you, that you are a child of God and He has made you in His image, and that it is possible and natural for you to be in communion with the Divine—if you believe that, you find your faith gives you power, because it *is* faith—it is belief in Truth. Be sure that you are praying to a God Who is your Father: that is the truth.

To what God do you pray? Purify your conception of God, be sure that it is as near the truth as you can reach in these conditions of time and space: and then when you pray your prayer ascends to God and is answered.

THE GOD WITHIN US AND THE GOD WITHOUT

TO-NIGHT I propose to close the present series of addresses on Prayer by thinking of that side of the subject which is of special interest to those who are accomplished pray-ers. I have been dealing so far with difficulties of those to whom prayer is not easy; but there are many people to whom prayer has ceased to be difficult, and it is of a certain perplexity which sometimes afflicts them—and which I am inclined to think afflicts other people watching them even more—that I shall speak to-night. You will find my text in the fifth chapter of St. John's Gospel and the seventeenth verse: "Jesus answered them, My Father worketh hitherto, and I work."

The passage that I read for the lesson, about Satan casting out Satan, is evidently one which made a great impression on our Lord's disciples. You will find it recorded in all three of the Synoptic Gospels, and it is developed and repeated and worked out in a very considerable number of figures. Those of you who are speakers or teachers know that, when you want to make a point very clear, it is no use just saying it once; you have got to put it in several ways, each of which elucidates the others, or impresses some section of your hearers. Christ constantly does this. When He wants you to realise what the Kingdom of Heaven is like, He gives you half-a-dozen figures one after the other: "The Kingdom of Heaven is like unto a merchant man seeking goodly pearls," "The Kingdom of Heaven is like unto treasure hid in a field. . . ." "The Kingdom of Heaven is like unto leaven, which a woman took and hid in three measures of meal, till the whole was leavened," and so on. He goes on using first one illustration, then another, and each of them makes his meaning clear and vivid to someone's mind. So with the saying about evil: Christ is desirous that it should be grasped, and it evidently was grasped, for each of the three evangelists have got hold of it, and in each case we find it surrounded by the same wealth of figures. "Every kingdom divided against itself is brought to desolation, and every city or house divided against itself shall not stand"; "And if Satan cast out Satan, he is divided against himself; how shall then his kingdom stand?" "And if I by Beelzebub cast out devils, by whom do your children cast them out? therefore they shall be your judges." "How can one enter into a strong man's house and spoil his goods except he first bind the strong man? and then he will spoil his house."

"He that is not with me is against me; and he that gathereth not with me scattereth abroad." And again: "Either make the tree good, and his fruit good; or else make the tree corrupt, and his fruit corrupt: for the tree is known by his fruit"; "A good man out of the good treasure of the heart bringeth forth good things: and an evil man out of the evil treasure bringeth forth evil things." One figure follows another. And again in St. Luke, Christ uses the same one about a kingdom divided, and entering a strong man's house. All illustrate the same point. It is a characteristic of a real truth that it is always true. If division makes weakness and disorder, it is true of good and evil—of God and the devil, and equally true of both. It is put from the other point of view in the chapter that Dr. Dearmer read from St. John, about the importance of unity. Our Lord prays again and again that His disciples may be one—"Thou in Me and I in them that they all may be one in Us." Here is the same principle applied to good. Division brings weakness, union brings strength and power. Is there not some deep unapprehended truth in those strange words which connect the fall of Man with "war in heaven"? Certain it is that wherever we can judge there is weakness in disunion.

You will often find in war that a great number of nations allied together are defeated by perhaps one nation or one or two, much fewer in numbers.

Why is that? Because the larger numbers could not hold together, and as soon as they began to quarrel, the weaker side became the more powerful. It is the same in industrial war. If this country had been faced last summer by the Triple Alliance of Railwaymen, Transport Workers and Miners, what would have been the result? It was because those three did not hold together that the miners were defeated.

This truth about the essential weakness of disunion finds its most dramatic expression when our Lord says "If Satan cast out Satan, how shall his kingdom stand?" but it is not yet sufficiently realised. There are many who do not realise that the power of prayer lies in the *union* of the will with God's will. When they pray they try to make God do what they think He will not do, unless they urge Him. Others are so sure that God is going to do everything that they rush to the conclusion that they need do nothing at all. I want to speak about them especially to-night.

We have arrived at a point where many of us grasp with faith the idea that God is within us—the belief that the Divine Spirit dwells not only in Christ but in every human being—the realisation that we are the children of God and, being His children, must have something of His nature within us. The sense of the wonder and majesty of human beings is the call to which many of us to-day respond.

But often the immediate consequence of that attitude of mind is what is called "Quietism"; the sense that one has nothing to do but to remain quiet and let God act. It is not a bad mistake perhaps in these days when most of us are so repulsively busy—when our minds are so rattling and banging that we do not seem able to be quiet. We do need to realise that God is working; that all we can do is to let Him work; and that we should be at peace. And yet it is possible to be so quiet and so passive that you become at last indifferent. There are people who are so sure that good will be done and wrong overcome that they cease, not only to be anxious, but even to care. It is difficult to bear in mind that love must conquer, that God is in Heaven and His love in the world, without losing something of that power to rebel against wrong, that instinct to fight against injustice, that is characteristic of our Master. There are people who are so removed from the world's suffering, so complacently sure that everything is all right and nothing wrong, that I confess they sometimes make me feel I would rather have any physical disease in the world than that mental disease of indifference to the world's suffering!

You have all probably met people who are unwilling to lift a finger to help the world because they are sure the world is all right. And here we touch the issue between the old teaching and the new. The old created often a conscientious, over-anxious desire to do everything, and feel responsible for everything: an almost morbid sensibility to evil which made the saint too like Shelley's "nerve, o'er which do creep the else unfelt oppressions of the world." The other extreme is sometimes not peace but indifference. People have said to me, "Why do you speak so much about sweated people? If you only realised that there are no sweated people, there would not be any! Why do you speak of pain? If you only realised that there were no such evils, there would not be any." That kind of quietism, I believe, is based on a misunderstanding of teaching about the power of God, and the necessity of union between His will and ours. "My Father worketh hitherto *and I work.*" If you have the Divine Spirit within you, it is a creative spirit. The Spirit of God is creative power, by which we are created and sustained in being: and if He is within us, we also should be upholding and sustaining and creating. It is because God is within us, that He cannot do without us. God *needs* both your effort and your prayer. That is not too bold a thing to say. He needs it because He chose to make us free. He put it in our power to choose wrong, to make war in Heaven, to create disunion between our spirits and His. He could take away that power, but because He loves us He will not. And therefore He needs the co-operation of the spirit He breathed into us. We must work with Him, and as He works, and with the same creative energy on our plane as He over all, "My Father worketh hitherto and I work"—and we work: that we too may be one even as Christ and God were One.

I think perhaps I can best illustrate my point by describing to you someone whom I know. Dr. Julia Seton, whose teaching I had the happiness to hear during the summer, is the personal friend of many people here, but to others she will not be known, and I think that she is the most perfect example I have ever met of that union which makes power—the union of her will with that of God. Such of her teaching as I was fortunate enough to hear dealt continually with the God within us, with the perfection of the union of the Christ Spirit with the human mind. You felt that she knew that all was fundamentally well, that she could not fear, that she could not doubt the ultimate conquest of good: and yet she was the most active and efficient personality that I have ever met. One of the most positive, most free, and most real. When she came into the room—and you remember how hot it was last June—not the weather for crowded meetings in stuffy rooms, certainly!—when she came in everyone suddenly smiled as though a light had been turned up in a dark place. There was no impression there of "passivism"; certainly no indifference or apathy; only a consciousness of someone intensely alive and active, though serene.

I remember one story she told us. She is a doctor, and she was about to go to a woman who was expecting a baby. She was called to this woman, who was four miles out of the town, when a tornado was raging, and consequently she could not walk. None of the cars were running and it was impossible to get a taxicab, yet she knew she had to be there. Well, I think some people who have great belief in prayer would sit down and wait for God to send a chariot of fire to fetch them. Dr. Seton did something very like that; she rang up the fire engine. It could not refuse to come out and she got it to take her to where the patient was expecting her. There is the real spirit of prayer! Dr. Seton was certain, absolutely certain, that it would get her to the place where she wished to go, but she herself looked for the means! Energy characterised everything she said and did.

Where, then, does prayer come in? Here, it may be said, was simply an exceptionally able and active woman, with whose ability prayer had nothing to do. Well, you can argue that, and it is difficult to disprove it. Yet Dr. Seton at one time was ill and weak and half-paralysed, so that when her nurse set her in a window and left her there, and it happened that the sun struck a flaw in the glass, so as to make a kind of burning-glass of it, the sun burnt her cheek, for she was too weak and helpless to turn her face. It certainly seems as if some energising power had entered in to make her the free, strong, effective person that she is now. It seemed to me that her faith in God had set her free. She was perhaps not cleverer or abler or more energetic than other people, but she worked entirely without doubt or fear or depression. She did not look for a means of reaching her patient on that stormy night with any doubt in her mind whether such means existed, and would be found. So she found them.

When you are free from any doubt about your success, when you know that you will find a way, all the despondency disappears. Your intelligence works clearly and without the lowering of vitality caused by doubt. My feeling about Dr. Seton was that her faith in God had set her spirit free and therefore she worked in that peace of mind which makes work easy, happy, effective. It is when one is in a frenzy of anxiety that one cannot find things, or bring them to a right issue. If you can imagine a spirit entirely free, you will see how it would realise that perfect peace for which we pray—that peace which passeth understanding, but which is a condition of the very highest activity. The divine spirit within is working with the Divine Spirit transcendent without. The Spirit of God is working through you, and therefore your spirit is creative also. It is indeed God who "works." What does a doctor do, but just try to remove the obstacles from the spirit of life, and let it work? The power of Nature is all he has to rely on. He cannot *make* life, but what he can do is to remove the obstacles—to reinforce the efforts that life is making, to take away that which hampers life, to get Nature to do the work that he himself cannot possibly do. But what an active co-operation is his! How positive a contribution to life and health! How far removed from mere passivity!

It is the same with the teacher. You cannot *make* the child's mind, you cannot alter the child's mind, all you can do is to give it a chance to grow, to remove the things that stop it, that spoil it, that divert it from its right development. But what an active co-operation that too is! That kind of teaching requires an infinitely more real co-operation than the old system of discipline. That attitude towards a child's mind, of letting it develop, requires an infinite degree of patience. It is the most real, positive, and active co-operation with the child that can possibly be imagined.

And so in our prayers, it is indeed God Who acts through us. It is the power of God by which all acts are done. He it is Who creates and sustains. But our part is not to be passive, to be unmoved in the presence of the world's sufferings. It is to move out of the path of humanity the things that destroy and hurt body and soul. It is never more than that, for God it is who does the rest. You and I cannot make humanity: God has done that: but the Divine Spirit within us cooperates with the God without, immanent with transcendent God. Our Father works and we work.

THE ETERNAL GOD

"Thou, Lord, in the beginning hast laid the foundation of the earth: and the heavens are the work of Thy hands.

"They shall perish, but thou shalt endure: they all shall wax old as doth a garment;

"And as a vesture shalt thou change them, and they shall be changed; but thou art the same, and thy years shall not fail."—(Psalm cii. 25, 26, 27.)

I WANTED to find to-night some phrase, some text or verse, that should express the human sense of the Eternal God; and I was struck by the fact that there was such a wealth to choose from that I could hardly decide which was the finest, or which the best expressed what I wanted to say. It brought home to me the truth that all human beings, whenever they become articulate, strive to express something of that sense of the Eternal which to our little, narrow, finite minds, seems such a strange idea—such an unfamiliar, impossible idea, for a little human brain to grasp—a little brain that reels at the immensity of quite little problems, such as the problems of this world;

that cannot begin to imagine such distance as science can measure whether of greatness or smallness, whether of time or space. And yet, although the wings of our imagination falter and fail so quickly, although the moment we begin to speak in millions we know that we have ceased to be able to understand what we say—yet the idea of eternity, the conception of infinite time and space, or rather the infinite transcending of time and space, is an idea which mortals, wherever they can express anything, try to express, and to which every artist, when he expresses it, finds in the human heart a response. That sense of the Eternal—

> "whose dwelling is the light of setting suns,"

that

> "light that never was on land or sea,"

that imagined eternity which the poet saw

> "like a great ring of pure and endless light,"

that sense of something without bounds, without limits, is so universal that every poet and artist, and musician, and prophet, and teacher tries to express it. And everyone who succeeds in expressing it even in part becomes the mouthpiece of all humanity.

The incurable home-sickness of the soul for God

is expressed in that great sentence: "The soul of man was made for God, and is restless until it finds its rest in Him." Do you know who wrote that? It was written by St. Augustine in the *Civitas Dei*— "The City of God"—that great book which was written when the whole world seemed to be crashing down in ruins. The fall of the Roman Empire was to St. Augustine and his contemporaries even a more complete catastrophe than the war through which we have passed, because, although to us it seems almost a little thing, it involved so small a part of the world's space, yet to those people, remember, it was the *whole* world. It was to them all civilisation—the thing that was like an eternal rock to them—crashing, when the Roman Empire fell. And amid the ruins St. Augustine began to write *The City of God* repeating the sense of Marcus Aurelius' great phrase—"The poet has said 'Dear city of Cecrops,' and shall not I say 'Dear City of God.'"

You and I have passed through such a convulsion, have seen all the old landmarks and all the old, stable things in a state of flux or of wreck. It must be possible for us too to rise, even only for an hour, above the battle-field, and to see that "Dear City of God"; to get again in touch with the Eternal; to understand how it is possible, even amid the wreck of time, to "smile to think God's greatness flows around our incompleteness, round our restlessness his rest."

I said that sense of the Eternal was in all poets and artists; but it is in you and me also. Even the Prodigal Son, whose idea of enjoyment was such a meagre one, *when he came to himself* said, "I will arise and go to my Father." And so all of us, I believe—every man and woman—has sometimes that home-sickness for things eternal, infinite—impersonal, if you like—for some God greater than any god we have heard preached, some God greater than any god that words can express for us, a God whose eternity, whose infinity, is to our fretted, disappointed, puzzled souls a rest, even to think of.

Now, we live in time, and so the moment we begin to speak of the eternal, we speak in terms of paradox, because we cannot think except in terms of time. I was struck when I was reading that little poem I quoted just now, with the paradox contained in the very words of it.

> "I saw Eternity the other night
> Like a great ring of pure and endless light."

"*I saw Eternity the other night!*" What has Eternity to do with "the other night"? And when I speak of the immortal spirit of man, I find myself saying, "Man is *now* an immortal spirit. He is not to *become* one, he is *now* an immortal spirit": and what has immortality to do with *now*, or eternity with the other night? But you see how it is. We cannot express the Infinite and the Eternal in any human words without paradox, because it is something greater than any intellectual formula can contain: it is something bigger than we can reach after with our minds. Yet we are always trying to find it, and always trying to reach it.

> "Life, like a dome of many coloured glass,
> Stains the white radiance of Eternity."

Our ideas of time, and change, and space, and personality—of all things—come to us in a cramped and limited way. Our brains are cramped and limited; our lives are so. How many people does anyone in this hall know? How many lands have they visited? How many planets have they lived on? We must be limited; in one sense it is impossible that we should not be.

> "Life, like a dome of many coloured glass,
> Stains the white radiance of Eternity."

You see Shelley's figure of speech? Light is white. The light in which you see truth is white. But, as you know, that white light is made up of seven different colours—seven different rays—and if you see life, or God, in the light of any one of those rays—yellow, or violet, or blue, or red, whatever it is—you do not see quite truly: the fact that you are only seeing by one ray of the prism prevents that. It is only when the seven are fused in the "white radiance of eternity" that you see truly, that you really see the colour of anything. And so I believe it is with our minds. We have reason and emotion, we have senses, we have how many unclassified ways of apprehending the truth? But when we seek for God, we must concentrate all our powers. We must desire Him with the whole of our being. And when the poet expresses for us God, he does it by some appeal which contains reason, which appeals to our reason, but which appeals to more than reason. We can never, by reasoning, say why that line from Wordsworth:

> "Whose dwelling is the light of setting suns"

seems to express for us the eternal reality. How can we explain it in words? We cannot, because Wordsworth is appealing to something more than our minds, including our minds, indeed, but transcending them: he appeals to the whole of our personality—our thought, emotion, memory, and senses—the recollected sight of setting suns, the emotions awakened by them, the sense of space and time and beauty. Our whole personality, *including* our intelligence, is reached by the poet in that appeal, and for a moment you see—not life through "a dome of many coloured glass," but "the white radiance of eternity."

Seek it with all your heart. This is what is

meant by that great sentence: "If with all your hearts ye truly seek Him, ye shall ever surely find Him." All things reveal Him to us when we seek for Him with *all* our heart. Despise no way. Do not say "such a man finds God in the wrong way, or in the wrong place—in some Church that we don't like." Or, "he never goes to church at all: he says he finds God more easily on the hill-tops or by the sea." Or "such another is blind to natural beauty—so stupid that he cannot see God, even in the stars. He only sees Him in the human heart: he is an atheist; he worships humanity." All these are revelations of God, and he is indeed half an atheist who denies any of them. And if there is anyone here who is ever stirred by the sense of the eternal, of something infinite and absolute, he has found God, and no one, of whatever creed, should say to him that he does not know God. Such men *do* know Him, even while they call themselves atheists, if they find that eternal beauty, that infinite harmony, anywhere in creation, and some find him in the glory of the sky and sea, and some in the great reaches of the human mind.

You remember that saying I have quoted more than once of Kepler who, when he studied the stars, felt that he was "thinking God's thoughts after Him." Would anyone dare to say of any great scientist who could feel like that even if he did not use the name of God, that he was an atheist? Do not you see that to recognise beauty, and wonder, and awe, *is* worship, and that if people worship God in any of these aspects they are right? Wrong where they deny Him, but right where they see Him.

Other people find Him only, or chiefly, in human experience. To many people, the last line of one of the carols we sang just now—which reminded us that though the angels, and the wise, and the poor, all came to worship our Lord, only His Mother worshipped him with a kiss—is an expression of the divine, for they find God in the touching innocence and trust of a little human child. And I have known such a man call himself deliberately an atheist, and I have felt inclined to say, but with a smile: "'The fool hath said in his heart, There is no God,' when he is worshipping God, even as he says it!"

But to have this experience when all the world seems broken and tormented does need that you seek for it with all your heart, and I believe that this is why so often very simple people, and unlearned people, people, perhaps, with very limited experience of life as well as of books, with very few opportunities of culture or education, in the ordinary sense, are so sure of God; because if we seek for God with all our heart, we achieve that unity which is divine. "Deep calls to deep," and it is when by our longing we are fused into one that we apprehend God, who is One. When we concentrate on the great search, as a scientist on truth, or an artist on beauty, or a priest on the service of humanity—when that passion of longing takes up all our power and all our being, we have in ourselves that harmony which is the quality of God. And so, perhaps for the first time, we *see* Him.

Now, if you have a very brilliant intellect, and you see a person more stupid than yourself who, nevertheless, is much wiser in spiritual things, do not suppose that this is because the intellect is a hindrance to seeing God. Your failure is due to the fact that you have never reached that unity which a simpler and possibly a less intellectual nature than yours has attained. It is not a question of the relative brilliancy of your intelligence. What is any human intellect, compared with the Universe? "Merit lives from man to man, and not from man, O God! to Thee." After all, how much difference is there between the greatest and smallest of us? But that quality which comes of developing all your powers—all of them—in the search for God, until in the greatness of your longing all are fused in the white heat of passion, that is a quality of God Himself. The simplest people can have it, and sometimes find it more easily than the more complex and warring natures whose harmony is difficult to achieve.

It is the pure in heart that see God, and that saying does not mean just those people who have one particular virtue, more rightly called chastity.

It means singleness of mind, singleness of heart; it means a desire for God that purifies out of you every other desire. That is the purity of heart which sees God. And I think that this is why children seem sometimes so easily to see Him. The absolute absorption, the extraordinary concentration, which is possible for a child, which is easy to him, which a child displays again and again in the pursuit of his play, or his imagination —is often much more difficult to grown-up people. We have allowed ourselves to become so distracted, so busy, so frivolous. But watch a child, absorbed, perhaps, in a new idea. Is there in the world a singleness of mind so perfect? Why, all modern teaching, I suppose, is an attempt to use that marvellous concentration, that intense absorption of the child's whole personality, in the interests of education—to transfer it from what is called "play" to what is called "work," to make of work, play, in the sense that the child will pursue it with the same single-souled absorption.

Where will you see such perfect concentration in a grown-up person? I will tell you where. You will see it in the saint, and you find it in the genius. That is why genius sometimes seems to the ignorant childish, and to the wise child-like. You have heard of the great French natural historian Fabre, who used to sit, perhaps from sunrise to sunset, with his eyes fixed on some little patch of ground, where he was watching the lives and the conduct of some tiny little insects. He used to forget to eat and forget to sleep; he used to forget how the hours passed; he was unconscious of everything else, until the light failed and watching became impossible. And people used to go by in the early morning and see Fabre watching the grass, and when they came back in the evening from their work, there he still was, watching that same patch of grass. And they used to smile indulgently at one another and say, "Poor old man!" They thought he was childish, that wise, that far-seeing man. He was not childish: he was child-like. In the capacity to forget time, to forget space, to forget the needs of his body, in his intense concentration on the one thing that he desired to see, he saw what those stupid, uninterested people who passed him by and touched their heads significantly, to show that they thought he was mad, never saw at all.

And in some sense that quality of children and of genius is the quality that is required of those who would see God. "The peace of God which passes all understanding" comes to those who are conscious of the eternal, even amid the wreck and crash of time. "The peace of God which passes all understanding" possesses them. That is why people who often puzzle the "orthodox"—who, perhaps, would find it difficult to give an account of themselves—have yet such a serene assurance that though evil seems to conquer, good must triumph; have such calm, that even in this distracted world, they are not distracted; do not, though their heart break for the sorrows of humanity, lose that strength to serve which only comes to those who are with the eternal.

It is for this reason that I shall always be grateful to those teachers who bring home to us the absolute nature of God. To me God is intensely personal. To me it seems that unless I had known Jesus Christ, I should know very little about God, and that little would not help me very much. It happens to be the way I am made. But I do realise that to teach this aspect of the Divine *always*—to make God not only *include* personality, but to be solely and wholly "a person"—is to forget that the doctrine of the Trinity, taught not only by Christians but in nearly all great spiritual religions, is an attempt to express the personality of God in terms that transcend the supposed limitations of personality. I feel that those who have recalled to us, as Christian Scientists, for example, have done, the absolute nature of the Eternal God, have done a great service to all who seek God under whatever name. To escape from the limitations of personality, to think of eternity as a "ring of pure and endless light," to realise that even those who deny the personality of God may still reach Him and do still reach Him under other eternal aspects—this was a great service to all those who seek for God at all. If we can once realise that, then, though we think in terms of time, and though we must always do so, and speak to one another in words that imply time and space, so that our very effort to express the Eternal falter and fails upon our lips, yet we shall be able to apprehend the eternal God whom we can never wholly understand.

That would set us free to use every power to search for God, to cultivate every gift to serve God without fear or anxiety lest truth should prove to destroy God, or be too mighty for our faith, or too cruel for our hope. We should be free to serve, free to look beyond the latest theory of the greatest scientist, to be no longer tyrannised over (the human spirit is so often tyrannised over) by the latest scientific hypothesis; free to take all that truth can give us, yet never to be the slaves of any one aspect of truth; to remember that both history and science deal, after all, with time and space, and that we must sometimes look at man *sub specie æternitatis*—in his immortal aspect; free to build to-day in 1921 that *Civitas Dei*, that "City of God" which St. Augustine dared to imagine when all his world of time and space lay in ruins about him; free not to care very much whether our gifts are great or small—for in the presence of the Eternal, what does it matter? The only thing that matters is that with all our hearts we should truly seek Him. And it would set us free, therefore, from the fret and fever of our little selves and make it impossible for us to be over-anxious about ourselves and our undertakings, and our hopes and fears, in the presence of His infinite greatness; free, above all, to understand and to make our own the meaning of Christ's words on the eve of Good Friday, when the world was about to crucify Him and to fling back the love of God, "Peace I leave with you, My peace I give unto you: not as the world giveth, give I unto you. Let not your heart be troubled, neither let it be afraid."

Printed in the United States
105991LV00005BA/95-96/A